# THE ACKNOWLEDGED LIFE

# THE ACKNOWLEDGED LIFE

*God's answer for times of uncertainty*

ANTHONY J. DIMAIO WITH VAUGHN H. WEIMER

Copyright © 2017 Anthony J. DiMaio with Vaughn H. Weimer.

All rights reserved. No part of this publication may be reproduced, distributed or transmitted in any form or by any means, including photocopying, recording, or other electronic or mechanical methods, without the prior written permission of the publisher, except in the case of brief quotations embodied in critical reviews and certain other noncommercial uses permitted by copyright law. For permission requests, write to the publisher, addressed "Attention: Permissions Coordinator," at the address below.

www.acknowledgedlife.com

Anthony DiMaio ©2017

Ordering Information: Quantity sales. Special discounts are available on quantity purchases by corporations, associations, & others. Contact the "Special Sales Department" at doubleriver@gmail.com.

The Acknowledged Life: God's Answer for Times of Uncertainty / Anthony J. DiMaio with Vaughn H. Weimer —1st ed.

ISBN-13: 9781975714864
ISBN-10: 1975714865

# CONTENTS

Acknowledgements............................................ix
Chapter 1   Learning About The Acknowledged Life..............1
Chapter 2   A Collision with Acknowledgement..................9
Chapter 3   The Invasion of Data.............................17
Chapter 4   The Rewards of Acknowledgement...................25
Chapter 5   The Knowledge Economies..........................33
Chapter 6   Facing The Impossibles...........................39
Chapter 7   How Acknowledgement Differs from the Law of Attraction.....................................47
Chapter 8   Good Seeds Yield a Good Life.....................51
Chapter 9   The 5 Relational Fields of Acknowledgement.......59
Chapter 10  Acknowledgement is Confirmed and Affirmed in Community.......................................71
Chapter 11  Acknowledgements & Mindsets......................79
Chapter 12  5 Mindsets | 5 Wineskins.........................87
Chapter 13  Releasing Heaven's Atmosphere....................97
Chapter 14  The Ark of Character............................125
Chapter 15  Acknowledgement, Our Slingshot of Influence.....141
Chapter 16  Invitations.....................................153

About the Authors..........................................157

*Dedicated to Carol DiMaio, the daybreak of my heart, to Dom DiMaio, a great man of unmatched courage and resilience and Mary DiMaio, my mother, a writer who wrote her best stories on the hearts of those who knew her. Also, to all those friends of BOLD Ministry.*

## ACKNOWLEDGEMENTS

*To Stanford Erickson, Vaughn and Joann Weimer, CJ DeSantis, Thomas and Wilhelmina Lydon, Laurence Briody, Craig Medwick, David Moore, Yvette Arrington, Charles Loving, Jr., Daniel Kryger, Tom Kay, Christine DeCurtis, Cindy Wong, Chris and Jenn McLoughlin and all of those who through BOLD Ministry have been part of this revolution of grace in my life.*

## Chapter 1

■ ■ ■

# LEARNING ABOUT THE ACKNOWLEDGED LIFE

It was 1998, and the Internet was white-hot. People were throwing money at dot-coms. I wanted them to throw some of that money at my client.

I was working as a media consultant on Wall Street. It was one of the most exciting times in the history of the stock market. I was on my way to introduce my client to get funding from Bear Stearns. At the time, Bear Stearns was one of the leading institutional bankers in the world: and I got them in! I knew that this was my big moment. I personally knew only one of the bankers, so this had to be God.

We walked into this boardroom and I felt like I was sitting in the White House. Wow, was all I felt. That was the high point of the meeting. It all went downhill from there.

It turned out to be a business mugging. These bankers pummeled my client for all they could get from them regarding their business model. They wanted to steal whatever they could. I walked out of that meeting destroyed. My client flew back to Florida. It was the Monday before Thanksgiving. They were a start-up. They had no cash. I was getting paid in stock. It was over. My wife, who flew for an airline, was out of town on a trip. I went home to our apartment on 20th Street. I sat on the couch and prayed. I felt nothing at first. Then the silence broke. It took a while, but I felt like I was in the movie *The Ten Commandments*. I heard inside, "Thou shalt not bow down to Bear Stearns!" He said it again, "Thou shalt not bow down to Bear Stearns!"

He was angry. You see, all of my experience, success and knowledge had led up to that meeting. It should have been the pinnacle of my career, but instead it became the cliff of catastrophe. My reputation, network, and contacts at the *Wall Street Journal* meant nothing in that moment.

I prayerfully asked, "What do I do?"

I heard one word: "Repent."

I felt convicted, like when you get pulled over by a cop who just asks for your license and registration. I was blindsided by my own sense of self-accomplishment. I earned this break. I prayed for it; worked for it; I put this all together. And now it lay in a million pieces on the floor. I was devastated.

I cried, prayed and asked for forgiveness and fell asleep early that night.

As I was walking out of the apartment, still feeling the effects of my spiritual head-on collision with God from the night before, I sheepishly asked, "I know you told me what NOT TO DO; but you didn't tell me what TO DO?"

I wasn't sure if He was going to answer me, but He did: "Go to the media." That's all He said.

I'll come back to this story in a bit, but I think the analogy for our culture is very true: we as Christians are driving down the spiritual highway of life doing 90-miles-an-hour.

In some ways, I feel that we are living our spiritual life as if it is some new app that we downloaded. It is as if we are living our lives saying, I've got this salvation, God. Thanks for everything. Love that Holy Spirit, but I'll take it from here. Thanks, Dude!

There is no Cruise Control in the Spirit-Realm. Salvation, this Second Chance, this Second Birth, is something we live through a constant fellowship and surrender to Him – EVERY DAY. Our new life in Christ is not a franchise. It's much deeper; the good thing is that God as a Father can't be manipulated by our persistent nagging.

## THE ACKNOWLEDGED LIFE

My particular collision with pride is not unique. It happens to us all. It reminds me of the time when a friend in my Bible study group, who had gone from rags to riches and back to rags, told us all about himself right before he crashed: "Who needed God, when I was!"

We've got too much information blaring at us in the face. It is too easy to get distracted by the mass of information we are expected to consume. Notwithstanding, believers must resist the temptation to become so distracted that we forget, or so deceived that we choose not to remember that the Spirit-led life is born out of trust in God and by Acknowledging Him in ALL OF OUR WAYS [Proverbs 3:5-6].

*The Acknowledged Life* is my own rediscovery of following and fellowshipping with God in this new world that has no maps. The anecdotes, the ah-ha's, and the understandings are only the beginning. I consider this book the first chapter; there will be others that will take it further, always with the objective of knowing Him.

But allow me to finish the Bear Stearns story: So the next week I went to a PR Newswire breakfast where a CNBC reporter was featured. There were about 100 PR professionals there. They all went up to shake his hand at the end and to pitch him on their clients' stories.

I stood on line. I was the last to get to him. It was just him, me and the waiters cleaning up. I am sure he was exhausted by that time. I also knew that my client wasn't ready for the big time; we were on the bulletin-board. That isn't even an exchange. So when I got to him, I began to tell him how he could improve his show by broadcasting from the New York Stock Exchange (this is before CNBC came to the NYSE). He looked at me and asked me about my client. I told him. He asked for my card. I gave it to him. That was on December 3rd, 1998. On December 7th, Monday, I received a call from the reporter informing me that he was going to feature my company on CNBC at 11 o'clock on Wednesday.

It was a miracle. It was a watershed moment. What was even more astonishing was that I wasn't the only PR company representing the client. But after that day, I was. The stock in 4 months traded from $2.50 a share to $60.

ANTHONY J. DIMAIO WITH VAUGHN H. WEIMER

## THE ACKNOWLEDGED LIFE
## LEARNING THE POWER OF ASKING GOD, "WHAT'S NEXT?"

*"...but the people who know their God shall be strong, and carry out great exploits."* Daniel 11:32

I find that when I struggle and plan and strategize to carry out the will of God, I overcomplicate it at best, and at worst, miss it completely.

You and I will be faced with hundreds of thousands of decisions in the next few years[1]; some will be major choices and others not so important. There is no denying we need 'a technology' to help us hit a higher percentage of those choices correctly.

Our relationship with God began with a choice, and will involve daily choices in order for it to flourish.

*The Acknowledged Life* is about getting our relationship choices with God right, every day, with a high degree of accuracy.

God knows what we don't know; so why is it that we act like He doesn't, or worst keep Him out of the process?

When I Acknowledge Him *"in all my ways, He will direct my steps,"* the Scripture promises. Today, you are about to make 35,000 decisions experts say; why not make the best of those choices and Acknowledge Him?

I will choose to Acknowledge Him everywhere and in everything. I will leave outcomes to Him as I Acknowledge Him and do what I believe is His will and His instruction.

*The Acknowledged Life* is about implementing a two-word prayer: "What's Next?" That prayer doesn't come from me; I heard it first from Rick Warren on a YouTube video.

Pay Attention: God wouldn't have surrounded us with so many questions, if He wasn't prepared to help us with the answers.

---

[1] It is estimated that an adult makes about 35,000 remotely conscious decisions each day. (Joel Hoomans, Assistant Professor of Management and Leadership Studies at Roberts Wesleyan College.)

# THE ACKNOWLEDGED LIFE

It is just that simple; it is just that profound. So if you are willing to ask, "What's Next?" continue on to "My First Encounter with Acknowledgement."

## MY FIRST ENCOUNTER WITH ACKNOWLEDGEMENT

It was the summer of 1980 – about a year after my 'Road to Damascus' encounter with God in the basement of a Brooklyn brownstone. I was ready to write my great classic play about the red-hot love affair between Maude Gonne McBride and William Butler Yeats, the renowned Irish poet. I was having lots of trouble writing about it – the fact was I was getting nowhere! I finally decided to ask God to help me write the play. That is when I got this very strange answer back. I really didn't think God talked back to people at that time. Prayer for me was like a messenger service: I put in the request and waited for an answer in terms of resolution. He 'told me' to "Write My play first." I thought, "What play?" I then interrogated Him, asking, "What's the plot? Where's it set? Who are the characters? How do You want me to write a play without any of this information?"

His response was, "Just start writing."

One reaction was, "God doesn't write plays. I am crazy. I am going to write a play about something or one that I don't even know?"

So I sat down at the table and began to write; and I wrote and wrote and wrote and did about 30 pages when I stopped. I found myself writing a play about John the Apostle and his Roman guard, Cicrus.

After I finished writing the first half of the play, I gave the play to my girlfriend at the time to read. I asked her to read a few pages and tell me what she thought.

Ten minutes went by and I asked, "What do you think?"

She told me, "I'm still reading."

Half an hour passed by and I went back in for the verdict. She sat there holding the spiral notebook in her lap and stared at me. Then she said, "You didn't write this. This is good!"

When we Acknowledge God it is like writing a play, not knowing the characters, the plot or initially where it is set…but somehow it all comes together.

When we Acknowledge God it is like what I did with that pen: I put it into my hand and began to write, not knowing that after I finished, the reaction would be from those who read it, "You didn't write that!"

She was correct; I didn't write it, I just transcribed what I was getting through the inspiration of the Holy Spirit. It was a very big lesson for me, one that I have to continually rehearse.

## *Chapter 2*

# A COLLISION WITH ACKNOWLEDGEMENT

## ACKNOWLEDGEMENT

Today I intentionally choose to Acknowledge You in this day. It's Your day; I am looking to do it Your way. Show me how to Acknowledge You in my interactions and understanding.

## KEY POINTS

* When I Acknowledge You, I am facing the Truth
* When I Acknowledge You, You have walked into my life AGAIN
* You own my playbook: I am ready, willing and able

Proverbs 3, verses 5 and 6 is an oft-quoted scripture and is a fitting setting for this jewel:

"*Trust in the LORD with all thine heart; and lean not unto thine own understanding.*

*In all thy ways acknowledge him, and he shall direct thy paths.*"

Acknowledgement is not a theory or concept; rather, it can act as the filter through which we discern the what, who, and how of this new world of data. Of course, the most important Who is the One who identified Himself as the I AM, the Creator and Sustainer of the universe – God.

For me Acknowledgement was a collision – a collision of my expectations, my fears, my insistence on controlling my life with a God Who didn't back down.

The playbook [God's Word] NEVER CHANGES; BUT THE PLAYS DO! And Acknowledgement is the way we are able to 'huddle with God to get the plays for today.'

**The only way you are going to start to hear God is to stop talking at Him.** If we are not hearing God, how can we be led by Him? The louder life becomes, the more still we must become in order to hear the Voice of the Lord.

Today, in the midst of great complexity, we might be tempted to ignore or deny the fact that we are in a struggle. Like previous generations who shared this struggle, we use Acknowledgement as the rudder of purpose to guide us across the raging seas of distractions and disruption.

This book is written to assist you in discovering and to rediscover Acknowledgement as one of the crown jewels of the Christian faith.

## A TRADITIONAL DEFINITION OF ACKNOWLEDGEMENT

To begin with, the word "acknowledge" is a verb, not an opinion or an idea. It is an actionable thought or attitude that includes all of the following:

1. To admit to be real or true; recognize the existence, truth, or fact of.
2. To admit one's mistakes, to confess or agree with the idea of declaring something to be true.
3. To show or express recognition or relationship.
4. To recognize the authority, validity, of claims.
5. To show or express appreciation or gratitude for.
6. To indicate or make known the receipt of something delivered.
7. To give permission to access or enter.
8. To take notice of or reply as to a greeting.

To acknowledge means to concede, confess, grant, admit, or agree in the idea of declaring something to be true.

Each one of these elements of Acknowledgement plays an important role in our spiritual alignment with God.

## ANTONYMS OF ACKNOWLEDGEMENT

1. Deny, Disclaim, and Disavow.

To disavow: to disclaim knowledge of, connection with, or responsibility for; disown; repudiate

## A NEW DEFINITION OF ACKNOWLEDGEMENT

Before writing this book, I found myself reading Proverbs 3:5&6 and approaching Acknowledgement the way a worker would use a time clock. I would punch in – saying something like "I acknowledge You, God" – as I embarked on doing things for the Lord: sharing the gospel, laying hands on the sick and praying for healing, or leading a Bible study. To me it was a one-way street. I Acknowledged God and then went on with my efforts, according to the procedures I was learning from my understanding of what God wanted me to do, without really considering God in the whole equation.

Then I began to understand that my faith-walk wasn't to be lived out according to a theological formula or set of to-do's we are told on Sunday. In other words, Christianity was never intended to be a religion; rather, Christianity is actually a relationship, and God personally gets involved.

**Acknowledgement in Marriage**: I dated a series of Christian girls in my pursuit of a marriage partner. I sincerely wanted to be married and I knew God wanted that for me as well…Scripture said so.

I had my list of all the right qualities to look for: Christian, check; worshipper, check; attractive, check, check, check. I thought I had all the right boxes checked but I failed, not once, and not twice, but I was actually engaged three times. The last one was devastating. I threw in the marriage towel. I even started putting my brother's name on my U.S. Savings Bonds, since I was convinced that I was unmarryable. I doubted myself. It did not occur to me to doubt my process.

Then I had an encounter with God one night. I was praying in my living room and all of a sudden I sensed the manifest presence of God. It was overwhelming. This was something I never experienced before. In my spirit I heard this presence tell me: "I love you." When He said that, I began to weep and weep. Again, He said, "I love you." I began to weep again. And then the third time He said, "I love you." At that point I couldn't take it anymore. I knew if He said it again I wouldn't be able to withstand it. I said, "Please stop. I know you do."

Then this voice said, "What did I tell you?"

I knew what He was talking about. We never actually had the conversation, but there was no doubt He was talking about my getting married, that finding and marrying a life partner was His will for my life.

I told Him, knowing this, "It's OK, Lord. I don't have to be married." But I still believed I was not going to find the right person, because I had missed my chance.

That is when the conversation got a little tense. He then stated, "Am I a man that I should lie?"

"No, Lord. I Acknowledge that You don't lie and that You will do exactly what You said You would do." I was left chastened but still very single and with no idea of how that would change.

The presence left my Brooklyn apartment. Yet, there was no denying God had invaded my life and my only possible response was to Acknowledge what He said as truth in my soul with words unspoken. Mind you, the Lord didn't make my future wife miraculously appear. No, it would require the cajoling of a friend to make me realize the person God had sent to me was right in front of me. Oh, and as it turned out she was a Christian, a worshipper and quite, quite, quite attractive… imagine that!

The Lord had to break into my life to break me out of the religious formula I had slavishly pursued to find my mate. It was His Acknowledgement of my earnest and appropriate desire that would result in my marriage to

# THE ACKNOWLEDGED LIFE

Carol after three failed engagements. This past summer, over 27 years later, when Carol and I visited my father, Dad said to Carol, "Every night before I close my eyes, I thank God for sending you to my son."

I learned Acknowledging God is a two-way street; it requires you give Him a chance to speak, and to act in your life. When God speaks, things change. Dramatically. That's how it's planned.

Another transformational encounter with the Acknowledged Life took place not long after our wedding. We got married and 30 days later I was fired. I had quit my job at the New York Stock Exchange and joined a headhunting firm prior to getting married. I thought the new job was a better career path.

After I got fired I decided that I should seek the counsel of my then pastor, AR Bernard.

When I asked for an appointment to discuss my life predicament, he sternly told me, "I'll give you 15 minutes."

That was big of him, I thought disapprovingly.

I went to speak with him, and after about 7 minutes he asked, "What was the last thing the Lord told you to do in work?"

I went through my career, and at each point, it was punctuated by God led me, or God opened the door. When I said, "And then I left the NYSE…"

Pastor Bernard asked, "Did He tell you to leave?"

"No. But it was …"

Pastor Bernard again interrupted, saying, "You need to repent."

My counseling session was over. I repented and had to acknowledge that I acted presumptuously.

Literally within a week, I was hired by an asbestos removal firm, where I discovered the Lord had given me a gift for marketing.

He showed me a pattern: Let God talk. Wait for Him to say something. Then do what He says.

Before – I would look for the formula, and then attempt to execute it without God.

God's not a formula. He is a Father.

**I began to see every famine in Scripture, as in life, is a setup, instead of a letdown.** It was a conspiracy of grace. I stopped believing out of need and began believing as a matter of trust, obedience and Acknowledgement of my relationship to the Lord.

Recently, in April of 2016, I began to see some simple prayers answered: checks in the mail when they were needed, a growth spurt in our ministry on the New York Stock Exchange, and even those people we were praying for began having fantastic answers to their prayers for healing, provision and deliverance.

Whenever I was intentional about Acknowledging God, things went smoother than expected. It wasn't like Liquid-Plumbr, but there was a decided shift in my peace. I wasn't passively sitting around for God. I was listening, asking for His input, doing what I thought He wanted and working on the projects He was directing me to work on.

Takeaway: I see the God of the Gaps as also Lord over them. The spaces. The needs. The losses.

Nothing is lost in God, except pride, addictions, and toxic attitudes.

**Home Improvement**: Another big Acknowledgement victory one spring was getting the two-story atrium-foyer in our home painted. It has taken some hits, especially from the effects of Superstorm Sandy, and the extra cold winters. Paint was peeling, walls were cracking and things were generally falling down around us. I needed to get things fixed and for a good price. But if you own a home you know getting a good worker to do a job can be a gamble at best.

I then Acknowledged God in my painting project. I asked God for help. I Acknowledged Him in all my ways… and that meant in my HALLways. Then I came upon a man and his dog who would come to the beach where I spend time with the Lord in the morning. Come to find out, Mike is a painter. I asked him for an estimate. That spring Mike the painter repaired and painted my hallway in 3 days. And for a great price (call me for Mike's number).

Most of life is spent in the hallways, going from one room to another. It's often the hallways that need a lot of the work. I think there is a very important lesson to be learned from my ordeal of getting a painter for my hallway: when you trust and Acknowledge the Lord in life's hallways, He'll always direct you to The Door [aka: Jesus]!

**Acknowledging God** is not like browsing a spiritual Angie's List. It's better. It allows God to become involved in providing for us what we need.

**Acknowledging God** can turn facing a lifetime spent alone into finding the perfect life partner.

**Acknowledging God** enables Him to answer our prayers, *"exceedingly abundantly above all we could ask or think."* Ephesians 3:20

**Acknowledging God** doesn't make you perfect or situations perfect; but it challenges us to stay flexible enough to keep moving forward.

Everything that "happens" isn't all good, but when we **Acknowledge Him** and put our choices into His hands, it turns out all God.

**Acknowledging God** reveals His identity to be God of the Gaps.

When we **Acknowledge God**, we allow Him to Acknowledge us and act on our behalf. Our life becomes an Acknowledged Life.

**ACKNOWLEDGEMENT PRAYER:**

Lord, help me to remember that You are not just the Lord of the breakthrough, but You are the Lord of the move through, love through, work through and pray through. Remind me that in my hallways, You are not rushing me along, but You are right there, walking with me. Thank you. You didn't have to do this for me; You wanted to do it for and with me. Help me not to forget and always to Acknowledge You in all my HALLways.

## *Chapter 3*

# THE INVASION OF DATA

## ACKNOWLEDGEMENT

Lord, You are good to me. I am not an accident, not a casualty or a victim. I am a redeemed, resilient child of God on a mission.

## KEY POINTS

* I Acknowledge that You have formed me and placed me by divine purpose
* I Acknowledge You into each of my fields: me, my call, talents and community
* You have provided me with the seeds to plant to produce an eternal harvest

Over the course of the last 15 years, especially for those on the East Coast, we have been impacted by a series of life collisions: the collapse of the stock market - twice, the devastating effects of the attacks on 9/11, two wars, multiple terrorist attacks, 4 major hurricanes and the worst recession since the Great Depression. As a result, millions of people have suffered physical, emotional and financial trauma, with the effects still felt for many years. But perhaps the most insidious attack, whether by land, air or sea, has been the invasion of data: we are hypnotized by those little devices in our hands.

## THE STEALTH INVASION

Unlike every generation born before the Internet, the sheer amount of information that has been thrust upon us acts as an assault on our psyches, having a multiplier effect on all aspects of our lives. The Millennial Generation is the first one that was born believing reality is virtual. Today, one of the most powerful engines of change exists in a realm the experts call the cloud. In this cloud exists a thousand quadrillion bits of data and information that deluges people simply as a by-product of their connection to the Internet.

For all of us in the developed world, we now take in 5 times more data in a day as we did in 1986! The impact of this data tsunami is the equivalent of reading 7 newspapers from cover to cover every single day of our lives.[2] We are a culture under a data siege.

Unfortunately, the thirst for knowledge has become unquenchable. Today's information comes at us with the force of water shooting from a fire hose, believing we have an unlimited capacity to drink in all of this data, but in truth we are drowning.

Data has gone from being a tool we use to a Trojan horse, invading our kitchens, trains, bedrooms, living rooms and classrooms non-stop. Information has morphed from being a springboard to achieving our goals to being an anchor holding us back from our destinies.

One thesis of the Acknowledged Life is we must be intentional and discriminatory about the data we ingest, since the flood of information that barrages us also threatens to inundate and obscure 5 critical areas of our lives.

---

[2] Chalene Johnson http://www.chalenejohnson.com/podcasts/how-to-organize-your-brain-creating-laser-focus-in-a-fragmented-world/

## THE 5 ACKNOWLEDGEMENTS

The foundation of the Acknowledged Life is built upon 5 Basic Acknowledgements:

Acknowledgement of God
Acknowledgement of ourselves
Acknowledgement of our destiny
Acknowledgement of our gifts
Acknowledgement of our community

Scripture tells us we perish for lack of 3 things: knowledge, vision and counsel.[3] Not just any knowledge, but knowledge from and of God.

## INFORMATION WITHOUT GOD IS DISRUPTION

Economists now see this sea of data as disruption, demanding that we create huge arsenals of supercomputers in the cloud.

In the last 150 years or so there have been at least three major events that have disrupted culture on a global scale. The first is the Industrial Revolution, which saw the world go from candlelight to electricity and movement being measured in hundreds of horsepower.

The second is the invention of the transistor in the 1950s that triggered a vast array of further inventions that eventually enabled space exploration. The third is the silicon chip, which ushered in the manipulation of data on a scale never before seen and led to, among other things, the Internet.

Just as the Industrial Age replaced the commerce and activities of the age that preceded it, and the advent of the transistor accelerated life for all whose lives it touched, creating new problems replacing old problems:

---

[3] Hosea 4:6 My people are destroyed from lack of knowledge. Proverbs 29:18 Where there is no vision, the people perish Proverbs 11:14 "Where no counsel is, the people fall."

* People feel more isolated than ever before.[4]
* The kind of bullying and abusive behavior that plagued people in the schoolyard has now invaded cyberspace, leading to catastrophic results.[5]
* Pornography and explicitly violent images that were once relegated to the back rooms of seedy establishments are now available for anyone with a browser, and innocence has become a casualty of the proliferation of this filth.

Acknowledgement is God's recommended prescription to deflect this deadly and disruptive barrage of data. I believe the degree to which we Acknowledge God will be proportionate to the quality of our decisions.

More than ever, our ability to Acknowledge God - which combines spiritual knowledge, humility, courage and psychology - plays an ever-increasing role in the navigation through everyday life. Acknowledgement is the 'spiritual dashboard' that allows us to receive and process information through God's spiritual matrix, which requires:

1. Hearing what God has to say (Jesus said, "My sheep hear my voice." John 10:27)
2. Understanding how it applies to our current situation
3. Acting, with faith, on what He has said

---

[4] Science bears this out, and an article in the business publication *Fortune Magazine* reported in June 2016: "The percentage of Americans who responded that they regularly or frequently felt lonely was between 11% and 20% in the 1970s and 1980s... In 2010, the American Association of Retired Persons (AARP) did a nationally representative study and found it was closer to 40% to 45%. And a recent study done on older adults out of University of California – San Francisco put it at 43%... (and also) loneliness increased odds of an early death by 26%." http://fortune.com/2016/06/22/loneliness-is-a-modern-day-epidemic/

[5] Ryan Broderick
https://www.buzzfeed.com/ryanhatesthis/a-ninth-teenager-since-last-september-has-committed-suicide/

## INFORMATION OR REVELATION

When God instructed Adam and Eve not to eat of the Tree of the Knowledge of Good and Evil, He wasn't keeping something from them. He knew such knowledge would prove to be catastrophic without the guidance of the Holy Spirit.

We still cannot handle a full frontal attack of the world's knowledge, which is why we MUST rely upon God's Spirit to lead us. The good news is that when Jesus' time on earth ended, the Holy Spirit was sent so He could finish the last stretch of this fantastic story of redemption. When we Acknowledge God, we hand Him the baton of our lives, and He runs the anchor leg of the race to the finish line.

God's primary tool for dealing with the ever-increasing volume of the fruit of the Tree of the Knowledge of Good and Evil is the Holy Spirit. Our access to the Holy Spirit assists us in confronting and unraveling this knowledge gridlock through Acknowledgement.

We know from scripture the Holy Spirit is our Comforter; He teaches us about Jesus, He indwells us and empowers us. However, one of the roles of the Holy Spirit, not usually considered, is Data Analyst, spiritually speaking. He alone is capable of organizing, categorizing and identifying information in such a way that it promotes Heaven's plans, purposes and timetable. One example of this is King Solomon.

David's son, Solomon, was renowned as the wisest man who ever lived. His wisdom was a gift from God that came about as a result of Solomon's Acknowledgement of the preeminent role this characteristic plays in caring for God's people. Here is what happened as it is written in 1 Kings Chapter 3:5-12

*At Gibeon the LORD appeared to Solomon in a dream by night, and God said, "Ask what I shall give you."*

*And Solomon said, "…Give your servant therefore an understanding mind to govern your people, that I may discern between good and evil, for who is able to govern this your great people?"*

*It pleased the Lord that Solomon had asked this. "Behold, I now do according to your word. Behold, I give you a wise and discerning mind, so that none like you has been before you and none like you shall arise after you."* ESV

*Later in the same chapter, the story is recounted demonstrating just how discerning and wise Solomon was:*

*16 Then two prostitutes came to the king and stood before him. 17 The one woman said, "Oh, my lord, this woman and I live in the same house, and I gave birth to a child while she was in the house. 18 Then on the third day after I gave birth, this woman also gave birth. And we were alone. There was no one else with us in the house; only we two were in the house. 19 And this woman's son died in the night, because she lay on him. 20 And she arose at midnight and took my son from beside me, while your servant slept, and laid him at her breast, and laid her dead son at my breast. 21 When I rose in the morning to nurse my child, behold, he was dead. But when I looked at him closely in the morning, behold, he was not the child that I had borne." 22 But the other woman said, "No, the living child is mine, and the dead child is yours." The first said, "No, the dead child is yours, and the living child is mine." Thus they spoke before the king. 23 Then the king said, "The one says, 'This is my son that is alive, and your son is dead'; and the other says, 'No; but your son is dead, and my son is the living one.'" 24 And the king said, "Bring me a sword." So a sword was brought before the king. 25 And the king said, "Divide the living child in two, and give half to the one and half to the other." 26 Then the woman whose son was alive said to the king, because her heart yearned for her son, "Oh, my lord, give her the living child, and by no means put him to death." But the other said, "He shall be neither mine nor yours; divide him." 27 Then the king answered and said, "Give the living child to the first woman, and by no means put him to death; she is his mother." 28 And all Israel heard of the judgment that the king had rendered, and they stood in awe of the king, because they perceived that the wisdom of God was in him to do justice.*

Under the power of the Holy Spirit, Solomon is able to cut through the data, information and deception not only to the delight of the true mother, but in demonstration of a power at work in him never seen before this time.

Another example of this taking place can be seen in the case of Gideon. When we encounter Gideon, a man who is so afraid of the enemies of his people, he is carrying out his chores in secret. He is confronted by "an angel of the Lord "who calls him "a mighty man of valor" and the Lord charges him to "'Go in this might of yours and save Israel from the hand of Midian; do not I send you?'" Judges 6:14

After several false starts and tests designed to verify the validity of God's request, Gideon finally Acknowledges God. What follows are a series of events that stretch Gideon beyond anything he could have imagined:

* Smashing his father's blasphemous (but cherished) altars
* Gathering over 30,000 men to fight the enemy
* Telling 22,000 of those men to go home when God tells Gideon he has too many
* Winnowing those men further down to a total of 300 to engage an enemy of tens of thousands
* Engaging the enemy with trumpets, torches and crockery and seeing them completely vanquished

Acknowledgement enables the Holy Spirit to do what only He can do and orchestrate such an encounter demonstrating a resounding victory with just a few men.

### ACKNOWLEDGEMENT PRAYER
Dear Lord, I Acknowledge You over all of my data, information and tasks. You know what information is important and which is simply a distraction. Allow me to see what You are showing me, so men may experience your extraordinary in my ordinary.

## Chapter 4

### THE REWARDS OF ACKNOWLEDGEMENT

#### ACKNOWLEDGEMENT

Lord, as I Acknowledge You this day, You are rewriting my life script.

#### KEY POINTS

* What the enemy determined for evil, You are turning for good
* You have the power to change my story into a History that conquers hell and conforms me to Your image

Mark 9:23, *"And Jesus said unto him, 'If thou canst believe! All things are possible to him that believeth.'"*

Matt. 17:21, *"And nothing shall be impossible unto you."*

The word "believeth" means "a believing one." The Jews had stopped believing in the Word. They had sense a knowledge of faith. They wanted to see and then they would believe. They were so spiritually exhausted that they believed only what they could see, taste and feel.

Jesus is not tantalizing us. He is not giving us a hyperbole. He is telling us the truth. He is laying down the law for the New Man. You remember 2 Corinthians 5:17, *"Wherefore if any man is in Christ, he is a new creation.*

*The old things are passed away; behold, they are become new, and all these things are of God."*

Wherefore, if any man is in Christ, there is a new specie - something new that has come into being. The old creation was a failure, a subject of Satan. This new creation, this new man, is a master of Satan and demons. The old creation lives in the realm of fear and doubt. The new creation lives in the realm of the new kind of Life (Zoe). Jesus spoke to Martha, *"If thou believest, thou shouldest have seen the glory of God."*

The Advanced Bible Course E.W. Kenyon

## THE NEW CREATION

What you believe will either get in your way or provide a way.

Kenyon was referring to Jesus' comments in John 14:12 where He said, *"Whoever believes in me will also do the works that I do; and greater works than these will he do, because I am going to the Father."* The new creation is a 'superman' able to do these greater works than Jesus.

Paul writes in the book of Ephesians 2:10, *"For we are God's masterpiece. He has created us anew in Christ Jesus, so we can do the good things he planned for us long ago."* NLT

Kenyon's personal discovery of the new creation brings with it the superior spiritual methodology involving godly choice, by an act and decision daily.

Later on Paul writes in Romans 12:1-2, *"Be ye not conformed to this world, but be ye transformed by the renewal of your mind."*

In this life, when we yield to God's plans and purposes, it isn't a negotiation. Sometimes obedience or Acknowledgement can feel like a wrestling match or a punch/counter-punch process. Jacob, when he was wrestling, he initially thought it was some sort of a man – that is, until daybreak, when the stranger was revealed to be the Angel of the Lord.

Jacob then believed he was wrestling with the Angel, but he was really fighting against himself and his old nature. At the end of the struggle, two things happened: Jacob's hip was displaced causing him to walk with a limp reminding him of his wrestling match. And second, he received a new name, Israel, which can be translated "Prevails with God," and the Angel refers to him as a Prince. Not only was his name changed, but also his title.

When we make a decision to follow Jesus, the old passes away and all becomes new. (2 Cor 5:17) **When we make a decision to Acknowledge God, what often results is a wrestling match**:

Between our old nature and our new

Between the things that we see versus the things that we don't see

Between attempting things in our own strength and Acknowledging God

## CONFIRMATION BIAS

Acknowledging God provides for us protection against confirmation bias[6] – the concept that we tend to favor information that supports our preconceptions. Confirmation bias has the effect of 'validating us' when we come across information that supports our theories, hypotheses and opinions.

Acknowledgement is ultimately the spiritual lens that brings truth into focus so that we may discern accurately the true state of affairs. Most often we are not aware of such biases, and consequently the admonishment: "... *lean not unto our own understanding. In all thy ways acknowledge him, and he shall direct our paths.*" Prov. 3:6

"Unfortunately, even though we know a lot about how biases like overconfidence, confirmation bias, and loss aversion, people still struggle to counter them in a systematic fashion so they don't cause us to make ineffective, or poor, decisions."[7]

**Acknowledgement attempts to unhinge us from "the gravity of appearance" into an atmosphere under heaven's governance**.

Living an Acknowledged Life is a lot like flying a plane: in order to overcome the law of gravity, the aircraft relies upon the force of a greater

---

[6] Confirmation bias is a tendency to search for or interpret information in a way that confirms one's preconceptions, leading to statistical errors.

[7] *Harvard Business Review* Identifying the Biases Behind Your Bad Decisions, John Beshears and Francesca Gino, Oct 31, 2014.

law - the law of thrust combined with the law of lift. The phenomenon of lift is so reliable that airplanes were able to transport passengers 37 million times in 2014.

Acknowledgement introduces the lens of truth into every thought and action. When we fail to do so, the following effects take place:

## 13 SIGNS OF THE UNACKNOWLEDGED LIFE:

* Work consumes all of life. You define your life by what you can and have done.
* You use people and toxins (drugs, sex and TV) to avoid what you are unwilling to face.
* You take rejection personally, and dwell upon other people's estimation of you.
* You are a poor listener.
* You feel good when you judge another person.
* You have become a drink, food, or material snob.
* You HAVE to be in control.
* Other people are intimidated by you.
* You like being the expert. You have a hard time admitting you are wrong.
* Being wrong is a sin.
* Being right makes other people wrong.
* You haven't heard from God in more than a week; month; can't remember.
* You are never good enough.

## ACKNOWLEDGEMENT TRIGGERS SPIRITUAL RENOVATION

Through the process of Acknowledgement, God gains a foothold into our lives, allowing Him to conform us to His image.

Acknowledgement, therefore, is something that calls for regular updates and upgrades. As we grow in faith and relationship with God, we must continually discover and rediscover our distinct gifts, callings, seasons and purposes.

Acknowledgement is a lot like spiritual rebirth where we discover how to reflect, repent, restore and regain all that we are called to be.

When we embrace ourselves as a new creation, living the Acknowledged Life opens the door to all the riches and glory that are available in Christ Jesus. In addition to securing our salvation, by living out the Acknowledged Life, we empower God to empower us to live our lives from glory to glory and to represent God's kingdom here on earth. The evidence of this Acknowledgement comes in the forms of:

## HIDDEN REWARDS OF ACKNOWLEDGEMENT

1. Humility
2. Authentic confidence
3. Stamina
4. Emotional elasticity
5. Mental agility
6. Vision
7. Educational endurance: the power to learn
8. Relevance in the midst of disruption
9. Constancy
10. Community

This list isn't comprehensive, but it's a great starting point.

## WHEN A PERSON IS WILLING TO ACKNOWLEDGE GOD, THERE IS USUALLY A THREE-FOLD COST:

First, we give up our right to choose what we think is the right and easiest.

Second, we ascribe the outcome to God.

Third, we willingly surrender the times in between the Acknowledgement and the fulfillment.

Jesus, being the Son of God, understood Acknowledgement like no one else. It is said of Him, *"Though he were a son, yet learned he obedience by the things which he suffered."* (Hebrews 5:8) **Your talents and skills don't exempt you from Acknowledging God.** No one had more ability and power than Jesus, and still He only did the things He saw His Father doing.[8]

An earlier example of Acknowledging God is Moses. Recall that Moses' first act of "ministry" was a murder of an Egyptian (Exodus 2:11-12), which forced him to be exiled to the desert. Moses' calling and conversion did not place him above Acknowledging God either. No. As a matter of fact, probably because of his calling, his crucible was more demanding than those he was called to lead.

Something that isn't discussed often in church is that the Jewish historian Josephus records that Jochebed and Amram, the mother and father of Moses, were concerned that the edict from Pharaoh – requiring all the male babies born were to be killed – put the couple under the knife, so to speak. Jochebed was pregnant with Moses at the time, and Josephus writes that they prayed to the Lord about what they should do. An angel appeared to them, stating that the child she "was carrying would deliver the Israelites from slavery." The angel also said that he "would be raised in a surprising way and that his name would last as long as the world." (Antiquities of the Jews Book II, 9:3)

This is a wonderful example of Acknowledging God: they had the child and for 3 months they kept the baby's birth a secret. When they were out of options, they placed the child in a basket and set it afloat in the Nile River. Moses is 'miraculously discovered' by Pharaoh's daughter and at the age of 3 is adopted by Pharaoh, according to Josephus. (Antiquities II 10:1)

But God's plan for the future Israelites was not to have their deliverer negotiate their freedom. God isn't the only one who doesn't negotiate with

---

8 John 5:19 "the Son can do nothing by himself; he can do only what he sees his Father doing"

terrorists! [LOL] Moses would ultimately spend 40[9] years in the desert, shepherding the sheep of Jethro, before the Lord would entrust him with the Hebrews. Moses learned how to shepherd his own decision matrix and confront his own confirmation bias, by no longer taking things into his own hands as he had when he murdered the Egyptian taskmaster. Now he was not only a man who had learned to Acknowledge God, but he became an Acknowledged Man, Acknowledged by God.

Moses' life puts forth the challenge: **are you and I willing to Acknowledge God in EVERYTHING AND FOR EVERYTHING?** I think we might be able to nail this down in about 30-40 years, give or take a decade.

You might consider speaking out this prayer:

### ACKNOWLEDGEMENT PRAYER

Dear Lord, Your sacrifice did it all, saying, It is finished. I believe that to be true and truth. I ask not only to be a Believing One, but I ask that You would reveal to me the faith and the knowledge that comes by faith so that as I walk this day, this hour, your purposes get released.

I Acknowledge You.

I Acknowledge I am Your victory.

Where there was fear, I Acknowledge Your faith.

Where there was sickness, I Acknowledge Your healing.

Where there was hopelessness, You have provided a destiny and inheritance that stands unshaken!

---

[9] Moses spent 40 years in the desert tending to Jethro's flock and 40 more years tending to God's.

## Chapter 5

### THE KNOWLEDGE ECONOMIES

#### ACKNOWLEDGEMENT

Today, as I Acknowledge You, my paths lead me to divine appointments paved with obedience and trust. I am sealed and clothed with Your power.

#### KEY POINTS

* As I Acknowledge God, I am enriched with the fellowship of Kingdom relationships
* As I choose to Acknowledge and align myself with God, His economy of love and hope emerges
* As I Acknowledge God, I accept that this mission may encounter temporary shortages but God will supply my needs
* As I Acknowledge God, my success only exposes my access to heaven's gate

With the introduction of the Information Age, the world has constructed its own knowledge-economy and culture, often with selfish intent. Whether it is when the people built the tower of Babel, constructing a means to reach heaven, or when we manipulate gigabytes of data using mathematical algorithms as a means to outperform the stock market, man endeavors to use knowledge to influence economy and culture.

## GOD'S ECONOMY INVOLVES A KNOWLEDGE AND RESOURCES UNSEEN

There is a knowledge unseen – that of God. This is what occurs when we encounter the blessings of God. He redraws the limits of our capacity - knowing that God is 'baking our adversity into a victory pie.'

Freedom is the by-product of living in the knowledge of faith, and faith walks on the unseen.

One of the facts of faith I gleaned from my walk with God is He will test you in your finances because He understands that unless we are freed from the love of money, we will never be truly free.

## TWO CURRENCIES REVEAL TWO ECONOMIES

The U.S. dollar is not the only currency. God also has a currency. It isn't printed on paper. It is imprinted on our daily acts of obedience.

God functions in the currency of Acknowledgement and Acknowledgement involves obedience and trust. U.S. currency is seen; God's is invisible. It takes courage and character to operate in the currency of heaven because many times the acts of obedience often take place when no one is looking, except for God. You just start seeing a spiritual momentum growing in your life. And that momentum may take years but once it starts, it is difficult to stop.

God isn't a masochist: He understands that we need things; things like food, clothing, shelter, love, and all those necessities of life. He has promised to "supply all of our needs." Phil 4:19 The problem arises when an apparent condition of lack presents itself, and we presume this has caught God by surprise.

## TWO PERSONAL EXAMPLES

The first example is about how some friends tried to "get God to provide for their needs." The other story is how I thought I was smart enough to put a deal together and I didn't need His help. Both were misguided.

A few years ago, a friend insisted my wife and I go to this healing service.

It was intense. There was a lot of talk about healing, but then a lot more talk about money. It got to offering time. Our friends were just recently married and they were in some financial straits. When the call to make a pledge and write a check rolled around, they made the decision to give $1,000.

They needed the grand. They allowed their need to dictate an action that God was not requiring of them. Instead of Acknowledging God, they were "purchasing a spiritual lottery ticket" based upon the promise of man. Carol and I just looked at each other as they wrote their check. They needed the $1,000 but somehow believed they could get what they needed by giving what they had. Jesus said, "You have not because you ask not." We let the bucket pass by and frankly couldn't wait to get the heck out of there.

Things continued to get financially worse for them, and they ended up being forced to sell their house. They were expecting this huge financial windfall by impressing God with their faith. I can't judge their motives, but I can say that personally, whenever I have tried working a system that I think is part of God's kingdom, as opposed to being obedient to His instructions, it doesn't work.

## I LEARN ABOUT GOD'S ECONOMY

The second example is about what happened to me.

It was the mid-90s and my business was going well. I felt like the Lord wanted me to give some stock I had to a ministry. I tried to dismiss it, but it was bothering me. I had one of my conversations with God; I 'explained to Him' that this tranche of stock was for my retirement. Then the idea came to me: "Who are you going to trust for your retirement,

AT&T or God?" If God were a lawyer, He'd never lose. So I gave it to the ministry. In the meantime, I was working for a public company, and as part of my compensation was paid in shares of the company. At that time, that company's stock was trading at 6 cents a share. But then something crazy happened. This tech analyst for Morgan Stanley precipitously decided to recommend this stock and it increased to 19 cents a share. It took about a year or so for it to increase, but at the time we sold it, those funds provided enough for Carol and me to put a down payment on our first house.

When we Acknowledge God, He transforms knowledge into action. He takes knowledge, motivates us to act, and our obedience to those actions can bring us to a deeper understanding of the purpose and impact of those actions. This understanding is translated: wisdom.

### TRUE INTIMACY WITH GOD INCREASES INDIVIDUAL AUTHORITY

Acknowledging God empowers you to trust God for everything, and I mean everything.

God understands what we need. However, we also have individual wants. The deception occurs when the fulfillment of the wants is delayed by circumstances and thus we are tempted to act on our own behalf, not willing to Acknowledge God in the gaps.

That is why it is so tempting to judge your well-being by the size of your checking account or stock portfolio or the size of your biceps.

God understands that we need to be secure; He just doesn't want that security to be found in anything other than Him.

**Dependence upon money for our security is spiritual alchemy.** Just as the ancient chemists tried to turn lead into gold, we will try to turn money into security and God into an ATM machine.

When we Acknowledge God, we become more secure than money could ever make us.

I have discovered that the average spiritual battle runs about a decade, but that shouldn't discourage you; the minimal spiritual victory lasts an eternity.

## ACKNOWLEDGEMENT

Lord, I Acknowledge You are my source of Wisdom and that You have given me Access to Heaven's Heart, Christ Jesus. Open my eyes, my ears and my mind to think Your thoughts, so that I may walk in ways that evidence the faith that created this Universe. I Acknowledge You in this moment, and forever.

## *Chapter 6*

## FACING THE IMPOSSIBLES

### ACKNOWLEDGEMENT

Today, I am not impressed, discouraged or defeated. When an uncertainty or an impossible situation seeks to undermine my mission, I will keep focused and ask for help. I didn't send myself; I am one who is sent.

### KEY POINTS

* I Acknowledge that I do not focus on the problem, but rather on the Promise
* I also Acknowledge that I am a learner, which makes my life a moving picture, moving toward God
* I Acknowledge You in all my ways, and You make my life a HIGHway, not a Byway
* Accept it: We have all been dropped in behind enemy lines

The sinful condition isn't just some talking point from the pulpit of a TV preacher. Sin is real: look at society, at the violence and fiduciary improprieties that exist in everyday life. Sin is a spiritually terminal condition. It is spiritual cancer, stage 4. Inoperable.

The serpent was aware of this. He knew if he got Eve or Adam to eat of the forbidden fruit,[10] God's crowning creation would be doomed. Satan knew if God's creations sinned, they would forever be banished from God as Satan himself was banished from heaven.

And Satan was definitely successful at deceiving Eve...for a season.

But God...

### LORD OF THE COMEBACK.

I have seen comebacks. I am a comeback.

My mother, whose heart had a congenital defect, was dying from her pregnancy with me. Doctors were demanding that she abort me. She said "No." They still shot her with anesthesia but for 3 days she lay there awake, believing that God would give her this son. Finally, the doctors, unable to perform their procedure, were forced to allow Mary to give birth...to me.

My birth, in some ways, was a comeback. Our culture is richly seeded with great comebacks. Maybe that is why I am such a football fan, because in football, at any point, either team is capable of a miracle, a comeback.

### REDEFINING IMPOSSIBLE IN THE NFL

And when you talk football, two of the greatest comebacks came at the hands of the same man, a second-stringer by the name of Frank Reich. A Christian, his position on the depth chart didn't stop God from putting his name into the record books of both college and professional football.

The greatest NFL comeback was a playoff game between the Buffalo Bills and the Houston Oilers played on January 3, 1993. The Buffalo Bills came back from a 32-point deficit to win in overtime, 41–38. To date it is the greatest comeback in the history of the NFL.

---

10 The parallel is that we were created to eat fruit, but it is the fruit of the Spirit.

## THE ACKNOWLEDGED LIFE

What is even more amazing is that the Oilers had just crushed the Bills on December 27, 1992, when they beat the Bills in the final game of the season, 27–3.

In this playoff game, the Oilers were killing the Bills – having a 32-point lead at the beginning of the third quarter. Bills starting quarterback Jim Kelly suffered strained ligaments in his knee during the previous loss to the Oilers, leaving backup quarterback Frank Reich to quarterback the team. In the course of this record-setting comeback, Reich threw 4 touchdown passes.

This was not the first time Reich had been thrust into the position of authoring a comeback. Some remembered him as the backup quarterback for the University of Maryland Terrapins. Reich replaced starter Stan Gelbaugh on November 10, 1984, and led the Terrapins back from a first-half deficit of 31–0 to a 42–40 victory over the Miami Hurricanes.

What you might not know is Frank credited the historic Bills comeback and his role in it to his trust in Jesus. In fact, as he was surrounded by all the microphones, speaking to the assembled reporters and all those looking and listening in on TV and radio, he read[11] the lyrics to the song *In Christ Alone*. The verse of that song says:

> In Christ alone,
> I place my trust,
> And find my glory in the power of the cross.
> In every victory, let it be said of me,
> My source of strength, my source of hope,
> Is Christ alone.[12]

Frank Reich might have openly Acknowledged God **after** his record-setting achievement, but I am convinced he, like my mother, lived a life of

---
11  Frank Reich. http://inspire21.com/stories/sportsstories/WhatGodHadPlanned
12  *In Christ Alone*; words and music by John Koch and Shawn Craig; ©1990 New Spring a div of Brentwood-Benson Music Publishing

Acknowledging God long **before** the big game. As a result, God turned the impossible into the possible.

Whenever we Acknowledge God, we not only give Him the ball, **but He gets in the game.**

## ACKNOWLEDGEMENT BUILDS BRIDGES FROM THE IMPOSSIBLE TO THE POSSIBLE

The concept of certain things being "impossible" is scriptural.

It's impossible to please God without faith. [Heb 11:6]

It's impossible for God to lie. [Heb 6:18]

It's impossible to live without being offended. [Luke 17:1]

The Frank Reich story just shouts out to me that **backups must attract God's attention.**

It says to me that we have a God who specializes in "impossible."

I believe that each one of us is born with an impossible mission or missions to accomplish. There isn't a single person alive who doesn't have the seeds of greatness planted inside of him. Some may say greatness attracts adversity. But **in an Acknowledged Life, adversity becomes the greenhouse for greatness.**

What parent doesn't try to plant seeds of greatness in their children? So what makes you think God is a worse parent than you?

He assigned Abraham to be the father of nations when childless.

He assigned Noah to build an ark to save his family and the animals before anyone had ever seen or heard of rain.[13]

He assigned Moses to liberate an enslaved nation of 6 million as a fugitive.

He assigned David to be king by catapulting him into royalty with his slingshot victory over Goliath.

He assigned Jonah to preach to an enemy nation, even after he was swallowed by a fish.

---

13  Dr. Walt Brown *"Did it Rain Before the Flood"* http://www.creationscience.com/onlinebook/

He assigned Jesus to save the world as a Jewish carpenter.

It's funny: when God gets onto something, there is little chance of Him getting off it. Present-day psychologists would likely diagnose Him as an obsessive-compulsive. Thank God for that. Obviously, impossible doesn't intimidate God.

To Satan, once mankind fell through the sin of Adam and Eve, it was impossible for man to overcome that physical and spiritual death sentence. Adam and Eve were mortally wounded, terminal, no hope.

But God...

God had anticipated[14] this crisis with a prescription called salvation that involved a blood transfusion, but not just any blood; it was the atoning blood of Jesus Christ. Man sinned, but Jesus paid the price for that sin, in blood. As Paul writes in his letter to the church in Rome, *"...while we were yet sinners Christ died for us."* Rom 6:23

That is the Good News. Christ's resurrection is the greatest comeback in history. God brought Satan's season to a close. God, Father, Son and Holy Spirit, accomplished the impossible.

**When we Acknowledge that atoning work, when we accept Jesus as our Savior, we allow the impossible to become possible in our lives.** Acknowledgement not only enables our salvation but fuels our transformation into the men and women God has called us to be.

So considering your impossible situation – why do you think God is going to change for you? If He made the impossible into the possible for Abraham, Moses, David, Jonah, and even His Son, what makes you think He's going to change now? God specializes in the Comeback Business.

## A WALL AGAINST THE WIND: SUPERSTORM SANDY HELD BACK

My friends are well aware of my story of the impossible having to do with Superstorm Sandy – the storm of the century. Ordered to evacuate our home just two blocks from the ocean at the Jersey shore, we didn't

---

14 Rev 13:8 *the Lamb slain from the foundation of the world*

have a choice or a chance. But we had a God. Before we left the house, my new tenant asked if he could sandbag the front door. I told him that would be great. That night we stayed with friends, listening to savage winds tear through the neighborhood. What are we going to do? What will happen to our home? Our home was a gift to us from God. Now would it be destroyed?

I asked the Lord, "Will we lose the house?" And I heard a Scripture, *"When the enemy shall come in like a flood, the Spirit of the Lord shall lift up a standard against him."*[15] I told Him, "If that is all You are going to give me, that is all I need."

He asked me to trust and Acknowledge Him. I did. The wind didn't stop blowing all night. I would have to wait till morning to find out if what I had heard was true.

The water came that night. We saw the waterline etched across our siding. It was above the threshold of the door. My neighbors had gathered outside of our house when we pulled up. It was like a wake at a memorial service. They all told me how sorry they were for Carol and me. The fish from the ocean were on our front lawn, along with seaweed and all kinds of debris.

I opened up the front door, expecting to see pools of water, buckling oak wood floors, and all kinds of destruction.

What I saw was the apartment was in perfect condition. Nothing. Absolutely nothing. It was saved.

I stepped out on the front porch and screamed, "Hallelujah! The house was saved. Thank you, Jesus."

The house we live in was given by God. God gave it. God keeps it.

## ACKNOWLEDGEMENT IN THE STORMS

As far as God is concerned, when it comes down to us, there are just two elements: Trust and Acknowledgement.[16]

---

15 Isaiah 58:19
16 Prov 3:5-6 *Trust in the LORD with all thine heart; and lean not unto thine own understanding. In all thy ways acknowledge him, and he shall direct thy paths.*

Acknowledgement reflects a Godly reliance; it injects God into the thing or situation Acknowledged. We are so used to relying upon ourselves, Acknowledging God feels a little gutless; however, it becomes the runway for Him to land in the midst of our situation. It is also the basis by which we come into agreement with God's plan at the right time and place.

**When we Acknowledge God in any area, we are speaking into existence an unseen reality and outcome over what is presently seen.**

When we Acknowledge God, we're not backing off what we need or want, hardly – an Acknowledged Life is one fully engaged with the purposes of God and empowered by the hidden gifts and participants in acts of glory; consequently, we are a threat to all opposed to the knowledge and Lordship of God, and this is when the 5 dimensions of Acknowledging come into play.

## ACKNOWLEDGEMENT

God, You have told us that every good and perfect gift comes from You, and that You don't lie. I Acknowledge that You are trustworthy. Even when I don't see the Answer, You are my Answer.

*Chapter 7*

# HOW ACKNOWLEDGEMENT DIFFERS FROM THE LAW OF ATTRACTION

This chapter is intended to quickly address an important distinction between the function and root of the Acknowledged Life. Today there is an enormous amount written about the Law of Attraction and even more recently, Mindfulness. There is a very significant difference between Attraction, Mindfulness and Acknowledgement. They may look like they work to deliver the same results, but this is not the case.

Scripture deals with the counterfeits of Attraction and Mindfulness through the parable of the Wheat and Tares.

### WHEAT AND TARES
*"The kingdom of heaven is likened unto a man who sowed good seed in his field: But while men slept, his enemy came and sowed tares among the wheat, and went his way.* Matthew 13:24-25

**Laws of Attraction**: The New Positivity philosophy that professes that by focusing on positive vs. negative thoughts, a person will draw more positive experiences into their life. Their belief is based upon the idea that people and their thoughts are both made from "pure energy," and the belief that like energy attracts like energy.[17]

**Principles of Acknowledgement**: Are based upon Trust, Spiritual Reliance, Alignment and placing ourselves under the direction of God through submission, sacrifice - and most importantly, surrender to the promises that God has given to us who believe.

*"For in Him all things were created, things in heaven and on earth, visible and invisible, whether thrones or dominions or rulers or authorities. All things were created through Him and for Him. He is before all things, and in Him all things hold together. And He is the head of the body, the church; He is the beginning and firstborn from among the dead, so that in all things He may have preeminence."*

Colossians 1:16-8

The Law of Attraction stands in direct opposition to the sovereignty of God. The Law of Attraction puts **us and our interests** at the center of all things, whereas the Principle of Acknowledgement puts **God** in the center of all things, and by doing so, we yield to His Kingdom and Will.

We don't attract things to ourselves since the sacrifice of Jesus Christ has provided us all we need.

The two ideas initially appear to be similar to each other since they are a means whereby we gain access to the necessities of life. But Attraction and Acknowledgement are not the same.

Scripture holds the two systems as opposing each other.

Both are the result of seeds intentionally planted by a person.

"Life is filled with choices, choices that affect us on an everyday basis in everything we do which means our everyday choices are not without significance," writes Hampton Keathley III.

Things get planted two ways: either by our words or actions.

Our motives will determine what kind of seed we sow, and whether it is of the Spirit or the flesh.

*"For the one who sows to his own flesh will from the flesh reap corruption, but the one who sows to the Spirit will from the Spirit reap eternal life."* Galatians 6:8

---

17 Wikipedia

The way the kingdom of God flourishes is revealed to us in John 12:42, *"And I, if I be lifted up from the earth, will draw all men unto me."*

As we lift up Christ, we are actually planting seeds, seeds that will grow and produce the fruit that we need.

There is also another element to planting in the Spirit and that is how the presence of Christ has the power to attract the things of heaven.

As Jesus is lifted up, there is a force of attraction released: this is the Spirit of Holiness.

Now this doesn't solve all the problems, because once heavenly attraction begins to occur, everything else tries to get in its way.

*"I find then a law, that, when I would do good, evil is present with me."* Romans 7:21

God's word is represented by the wheat, which in spite of being infiltrated by the tares, is cared for by the farmer, and ultimately bears the intended crop.

Wheat is our potential destiny in Christ.

Wheat is our place in the community.

Wheat is the fruit that is produced when we are connected to the vine.

*"Ye shall know them by their fruits. Do men gather grapes of thorns, or figs of thistles? Even so every good tree brings forth good fruit; but a corrupt tree brings forth evil fruit"* Matthew 7:16-17

"Sow a thought and you reap an action;

Sow an act and you reap a habit;

Sow a habit and you reap a character;

Sow a character and you reap a destiny." Ralph Waldo Emerson

Emerson didn't invent this concept; it originated in the Gospel of Matthew.

Acknowledgement is how God graduates us from seeds of faith to the trees of inheritance.

## Chapter 8

## GOOD SEEDS YIELD A GOOD LIFE

### ACKNOWLEDGEMENT

Wow, God. When I Acknowledge You, I see such value and meaning in everything. I see clearly.

### KEY POINTS

* I avoid the temptation to rush Your timing
* I choose to sow and reap in the seasons of the Spirit, not of the flesh
* When I Acknowledge You, I move in Your kairos[18] timing within each season
* Your correction becomes a gift to me as I Acknowledge Your commitment and love

---

18 A time when conditions are right for the accomplishment of a crucial action: the opportune and decisive moment.

ANTHONY J. DIMAIO WITH VAUGHN H. WEIMER

# THE ACKNOWLEDGEMENT GUIDE TO FIELDS AND PLANTING

*Another parable put he forth unto them, saying, The kingdom of heaven is likened unto a man which sowed good seed in his field.* Mat 13:24

### GOD IS A FARMER

Jesus tells us that His Father is a Farmer: *"I am the true vine, and my Father is the farmer."* John 15:1 And even from the beginning of the Scriptures, we learn that Adam and Eve were originally created as people who would depend upon farming as not only a livelihood but as seasonal symbols to characterize the seasons of their lives.

Farming is not just an occupation in the Bible; it is a spiritual metaphor that characterizes life in the Spirit. Farmers inherently understand the principle we call Sowing and Reaping. Farmers live by this universal law: You plant seeds in order to grow and reap a harvest in the future. This agrarian model was perhaps the most effective force in the world for millennia until we entered, first, the Industrial Age in the mid-19$^{th}$ century and then the Information Age in the latter 20$^{th}$ century.

We are at least two generations removed from a time when life's rhythms paralleled the four-seasons of a farm. Now we set our schedules according to stock markets, holiday parades and commutation schedules instead of planting and reaping.

As our knowledge-driven economy intensifies so does the distance between the agrarian and the digital economies, erasing the relevant principles between seed-time and harvest. Seasons, times, seeds, and fields have become 'historical colloquialisms' as opposed to reflecting the processes of incubation. Still, fragments of the old lexicon still remain present in our language: people today when inquiring about occupation still ask, "What **field of work are you in?**" Field is from the agrarian lexicon.

As we have lost touch with the seasonality and rhythms of sowing and reaping, we are most likely going to need to reeducate ourselves. Coding is the 'new planting' of this generation. Unfortunately, a code doesn't reflect many of life's rhythms and delays.

Consequently, we misinterpret the delays in our world as problems instead of processes: AKA germination.[19] These processes involve phases such as beginnings, middles and completions (harvests). From the point of conception to manifestation exist periods in which the invisible processes of transformation take place.

The bottom line is people don't know how to wait. They demand it now, on their schedules of convenience. As believers, Jesus attempts to put us back on and into God's timetable and ecology, which is based on the agrarian model as presented in the parables:

> The waiting periods that must take place between planting and harvesting,
> The uncertainty of the abundance of the output,
> The importance of the quality of the soil, and
> The dependence on things not in our power to control, like rainfall and sunlight.[20]

The rediscovery of these processes and principles of sowing and reaping are fundamental precepts of Acknowledgement.

## THE FIELDS OF LIFE - ALL RELATIONSHIPS GO THROUGH SEASONS

The same sequence that occurs in the agrarian setting – plowing, planting, cultivation and harvesting – can also be found in relationships. It is important to remember we can't switch the order of the process.

Anything that attempts to interrupt the sequence of sowing and reaping results in a violation of nature.

---

19 Process theory holds that if an outcome is to be reproduced, so too must the process which originally created it, and that there are certain constant necessary conditions for the outcome to be reached. Wikipedia
20 Rainfall is a metaphor for the Holy Spirit and sunlight points to Jesus, the Light of the world.

While we cannot interfere with or shortcut the sowing and reaping process, or control the timing factor, I believe we CAN affect the size of the outcome. This is seen in both the Old and New Testaments:

*"Then Isaac sowed in that land, and received in the same year a hundredfold: and the LORD blessed him."* Gen 21:12
*"And other fell on good ground, and sprang up, and bearing fruit a hundredfold."* Luke 8:8a

By Acknowledging God in any area of our lives, we draw in and draw upon the benefit of "seeing things" from heaven's perspective and that perspective allows us to discern the field, the season, the crop and the harvest.

Acknowledgement enables us to press into those seasons[21] of growth with the appropriate spiritual endurance. Two of David's Psalms are wonderful examples of this: Psalm 23, Psalm 51.

## GROWTH THROUGH ACKNOWLEDGEMENT

In the same way that a parent can't make a child grow physically, neither can they enforce emotional, spiritual and intellectual growth as well. Growth is an outcome of what you eat, what you do and the things that you don't do. It is within this crucible of growth that often the relationship between the child and the parent is forged and established. **Spiritually, Acknowledgement is the humility that activates the inner "seed of potential" that leads to growth. Acknowledgement, thankfully also involves correction that leads to proper course direction.**

## ACKNOWLEDGEMENT AND CALLING

It was when David was a shepherd for his father in the fields that he encountered an aspect of God's identity: that of shepherd. It was that

---

21 According to Ecclesiastes 3, there are 28 seasons, plus two more, the season to repent and to remember.

understanding and experiential knowledge that would forever transform and characterize the relationship between God and His people once David became Israel's king.

It was by and through David's confidence, born through his interactional relationship with God, that he was able to pen the most famous Psalm 23. And so this shepherd boy became the handpicked victor by defeating Israel's enemy, Goliath, the Philistines' military champion, with a sling, a stone and a psalm.

## ACKNOWLEDGEMENT AND CORRECTION

Perhaps scripture's greatest example of Acknowledgement did not come with the defeat of Goliath but in that account of repentance for David's complicit murder of Uriah and adultery with Bathsheba.

After committing adultery with Bathsheba, the wife of one of the soldiers in his army, his conspiracy to murder her husband appears to have worked, except it seems that God saw the whole thing. Even through this most heinous act, God finds a way to bring some 'good' out of it.

David's personal conviction of this grievous sin led him to author his Acknowledgement of the wrong, before the nation and to believers through the centuries. His Acknowledgement and repentance offers a clear roadmap of contrition to all believers to follow for spiritual restoration.

## RELATIONSHIPS AND THE RIGHT SOIL

In Psalm 51, David chronicles his road of repentance, reconciliation and redemption and thereby delivers a template to those who fall short of God's intentions and grace.

## EVERY RELATIONSHIP REQUIRES A SPIRITUAL SOIL

According to the parable of the soils, there are 4 conditions of soil that correspond to the state of the human heart: hard, rocky, thorny and good.

The spiritual soils of the heart can be cultivated if we are willing and able to recognize its condition. Acknowledgement opens up our spiritual eyes, so that we are able to diagnose our own circumstance.

**Hard Soil**: This is the kind of ground or dirt that has typically been stepped on and walked on for years. It might even represent people who have been downtrodden. In this kind of soil, seeds are never given a chance to grow because, as Jesus tells us, Satan comes immediately to steal it before they can take root. I find it interesting that Satan wastes no time.

The first step to turn **Hard Soil to Good Soil** is to break it up.

*"For thus saith the LORD to the men of Judah and Jerusalem, Break up your fallow ground, and sow not among thorns."* Jeremiah 4:3

*"Sow to yourselves in righteousness, reap in mercy; break up your fallow ground: for it is time to seek the LORD, till he come and rain righteousness upon you."* Hos 10:12

**Rocky Soil**: It is incumbent for us to remove the rocks of offense, trouble or unforgiveness that prevent seeds from taking root. This process involves Acknowledging God's sovereignty as our Judge. It is up to Him and Him alone to restore the things that have been stolen from us and to punish our persecutors. If we continue to hold onto the transgressions of others, the rocks will remain in our soil. *"If you forgive the sins of any they are forgiven them; if you retain the sins of any they are retained."* John 20:23 NJKV

**Thorny Soil**: The seeds in thorny ground are choked by weeds, which Jesus says represent anxiety, fearful care and deceit. How do we pull these weeds up by the root? When Acknowledge God, we do so knowing that He is not the author of fear[22] and take Paul's prescription for anxiety.

*Be anxious for nothing, but in everything by prayer and supplication, with thanksgiving, let your requests be made known to God.* Phil 4:6

**Good Soil**: Rich, fertilized, and free from rocks and thorny weeds.[23]

---

22 2 Tim 1:7 *For God has not given us a spirit of fear, but of power and of love and of a sound mind.* NKJV
23 Coincidently, I don't think it is an accident that God made man out of earth.

It is important to note here, there is a difference between dirt and soil. Dirt connotes negativity; it is something that covers or veils another object. Dirt carries with it a sense of uncleanness and ungodliness. Soil, on the other hand, is layer of earth in which plants easily grow because of the compost of decayed organic material. The decaying matter acts as fertilizer enabling the soil to become a ideal medium for growth. So the soil plus water activates the vital elements resident within the seeds planted to produce the fruit-bearing plant.

Soil also played an important role in one of Jesus' healing miracles:

*As he went along, he saw a man blind from birth. 2 His disciples asked him, "Rabbi, who sinned, this man or his parents, that he was born blind?"*

*3 "Neither this man nor his parents sinned," said Jesus, "but this happened so that the works of God might be displayed in him. 4 As long as it is day, we must do the works of him who sent me. Night is coming, when no one can work. 5 While I am in the world, I am the light of the world."*

*6 After saying this, he spit on the ground, made some mud with the saliva, and put it on the man's eyes. 7 "Go," he told him, "wash in the Pool of Siloam" (this word means "Sent"). So the man went and washed, and came home seeing.* John 9:1-7 NIV

## Chapter 9

# THE 5 RELATIONAL FIELDS OF ACKNOWLEDGEMENT

In the same way that a farmer doesn't grow crops, he simply plants them, Acknowledgement is our "through Christ" pattern[24] of sowing that releases God into the 5 relational fields of our lives:

God
Ourselves
Calling/Destiny
Talent/Gifts
Community

---

[24] The phrase "through Christ" occurs just 5 times in Scripture: 2Co 3:4 *And such trust have we through Christ to God-ward*:
Gal 4:7 *Wherefore thou art no more a servant, but a son; and if a son, then an heir of God through Christ.*
Eph 2:7 *That in the ages to come he might show the exceeding riches of his grace in his kindness toward us through Christ Jesus.*
Phil 4:7 *And the peace of God, which passes all understanding, shall keep your hearts and minds through Christ Jesus.*
Phil 4:13 *I can do all things through Christ which strengthens me.*

## EVERY RELATIONSHIP IS A FIELD
Each one of these 5 relational fields requires its own appropriate seed and cultivation. The first field is our relationship with God, and it is God's touch that causes each of the other relational fields to grow.

Field growth, or rather, crop growth, isn't automatic; and so it is true with relationships. Jesus, in the book of Revelation, tells us the cure for relational dissonance is repentance and renewal, specifically returning to our first love. We can't teach relationship any more than we can teach love – it must be encountered, Acknowledged, and nurtured before there can be a harvest.

## CHRISTIANITY: A CALL TO RELATIONALLY KNOW GOD
*Not everyone who says to Me, 'Lord, Lord,' shall enter the kingdom of heaven, but he who does the will of My Father in heaven. Many will say to Me in that day, 'Lord, Lord, have we not prophesied in Your name, cast out demons in Your name, and done many wonders in Your name?' And then I will declare to them, 'I never knew you; depart from Me, you who practice lawlessness!'* Matthew 7:21-23 NKJV

Do you know Him? What strikes me is how Jesus called-out those who based their relationship on works done in His name without knowing Him. He described them as practicing a form of lawlessness. **Go figure?**

One of the greatest examples of Acknowledging God and knowing God is Eric Liddell. Liddell demonstrated knowledge and relationship with God. It became the subject of the Oscar-winning 1981 film *Chariots of Fire*.

The movie featured the life of Eric Henry Liddell. Liddell was born on January 16, 1902 and died February 2, 1945. He was a Scottish athlete, rugby union international player, and missionary, who chose between his religious beliefs and competing in an Olympic race.

The movie centered on Liddell's experience and actions at the 1924 Summer Olympics in Paris. Liddell refused to run in the heats for the race he had trained for, the 100 meters, because they were on a Sunday.

His faith caused him to believe that he should not participate in the race. Instead he chose to compete in the 400-meter race, which he won. He returned to China in 1925 to serve as a missionary teacher. Aside from two furloughs in Scotland, he remained in China until his death in a Japanese civilian internment camp in 1945.

His sister, a devout believer, challenged Liddell to give up running and concentrate on the call of God on his life to pursue his missionary work. His response to her, "I believe God made me for a purpose, but He also made me fast. And when I run I feel His pleasure."

What is personally of interest to me is the fact that this movie was released in 1981, and despite all of its clear religious themes, **it overwhelmingly won the Oscar for Best Picture.**[25]

## THE FIRST FIELD: GOD

*"For the just shall live by faith. For God's wrath is revealed from heaven against all godlessness and unrighteousness of people who by their unrighteousness suppress the truth, since what can be known about God is evident among them, because God has shown it to them. For His invisible attributes, that is, His eternal power and divine nature have been clearly seen since the creation of the world, being understood through what He has made. As a result, people are without excuse.* **For though they knew God, they did not glorify Him as God or show gratitude.**[26] *Instead, their thinking became nonsense, and their senseless minds were darkened. Claiming to be wise, they became fools."* Romans 1:17-22

## GOD IS TRYING TO GET US TO LOOK UP

Every day begins in the dark and that is why every day we need the light of the Son. It is not a one-time event. Yesterday's light is gone. I need today's

---

25 Not only did *Chariots of Fire* win for Best Picture, but also won 3 other awards, including Best Screenplay, and earned a total of 12 nominations.
26 Gratitude is an expression of Acknowledgement

light. That is why Acknowledgement is such a critical aspect of living out the life that God has given to us in the now.

**Like it or not, we are responsible for what kind of relationship we have with God.** A lot of us don't want to deal with the 'God issue.' Religion brings out the beads, burkas, the yoga, and whatever you plug in there, except for God.

According to Paul, God made Himself un-ignorable by virtue of Creation, and yet we have 'created' universities to 'explain' our way out of Acknowledging there is a God. Yet, He persists in trying to get our attention.

In the first chapter of Romans, Paul covers this first complication I call spiritual avoidance when he writes, *"They did not glorify Him as God or show gratitude."*

They refused to Acknowledge Him, and not because He was 'hiding.' Paul clearly states, *"God has shown it to them. For His invisible attributes, that is, His eternal power and divine nature have been clearly seen since the creation of the world, being understood through what He has made."* Rom 1:20

Acknowledgement will require us to make changes in the way that we do things and the way that we see things. We naturally tend to do what we want and then believe it to be right. *Every man's way is right in his own eyes; But the LORD weighs the hearts. Proverbs 21:2.*

All obedience must begin with a willingness to listen and then trust. That is why prayers of Acknowledgement differ from meditation or contemplation. Acknowledgement opens the heart's door to what God is saying that day. Some believe God has said everything He is going to say, and it's called The Bible. But the Lord is our Shepherd, and Jesus says about the sheep, that they hear His voice, that implies that He is still speaking and is STILL SPEAKING through the Holy Spirit. *"But the Helper, the Holy Spirit, whom the Father will send in my name, he will teach you all things and bring to your remembrance all that I have said to you."* John 14:26

## THE SECOND FIELD: OURSELVES

*"We are his workmanship, created in Christ."* Ephesians 2:10

We are not part of God's spiritual antique collection; something He collects and saves and He then places on some spiritual display case to admire.

*"All scripture is God-breathed and is useful for instruction, for conviction, for correction, and for training in righteousness, so that the man of God may be complete, fully equipped for every good work."* 2 Timothy 3:17

We weren't just saved; we were rescued and destined for a purpose. The moment the rescue took place, God issued us a new spiritual passport because He had plans for us. The redeemed people all have assignments and spiritual passports.

*"Now may the God of peace, who through the blood of the eternal covenant brought back from the dead our Lord Jesus, the great Shepherd of the sheep, equip you with every good thing to do His will. And may He accomplish in us what is pleasing in His sight through Jesus Christ, to whom be glory forever and ever. Amen."* Hebrews 13:21

We were all rescued for such a time and place as this!

In order for us to fully function in the specificity and capacity God wills for us, I found the following 3 Psalms necessary to review to maintain our identity, and calling in Christ:

Psalm 51: A psalm of repentance and contrition
Psalm 1: A psalm of instruction and edification
Psalm 23: A psalm of covenant and guidance

**Psalm 51** reflects upon our Acknowledgement of our sin. We are not victims, we are fallen. There is a big difference. The good news is Jesus knew we were lost.

God's prescription: Acknowledge our sin.

His solution: The salvation event of the second birth through Jesus.

I like what Graham Cooke wrote in his book *Divine Confrontation* – "Repentance is a continual submission to the revelation of the Lordship of Christ." If we allow ourselves to interfere with God, we have, for all intents and purposes, pushed Him aside.[27]

We need to be mindful that if our success hinges upon us and not God, we have edged Him out, and as everyone knows, EGO stands for Edging God Out.

**Psalm 1** reinforces how the first act of Acknowledging God is to stop. Stop doing. Stop striving. Stop litigating. Stop justifying and acquitting your own failures. Stop trying to do your life without Him.

Psalm 1 places an immediate hold on the man who is blessed.

The writer cautions the readers to put a halt to walking in the counsel of the wicked [Proverbs 3:5 Lean not to your own understanding]; getting in the way of sinners [versus having the Lord direct your steps]; and sitting in the seat of scoffers [versus trusting in the Lord]. And then, the Psalmist instructs the blessed man to get planted and stay planted, growing into His destiny.

1. *Blessed is the man who walks not in the counsel of the wicked, nor stands in the way of sinners, nor sits in the seat of scoffers;*
2. *but his delight is in the law of the Lord, and on his law he meditates day and night.*
3. *He is like a tree planted by streams of water that yields its fruit in its season, and its leaf does not wither. In all that he does, he prospers.*
4. *The wicked are not so, but are like chaff that the wind drives away.*
5. *Therefore the wicked will not stand in the judgment, nor sinners in the congregation of the righteous;*
6. *for the Lord knows the way of the righteous, but the way of the wicked will perish.*

**Psalm 23:** I view Psalm 23 as behavioral therapy.

---

27 *Divine Confrontation* p. 66, Graham Cooke

This is the final stage of Acknowledgement: our pursuit of the Shepherd. Remember, Jesus is described as being not just any shepherd, but the Good Shepherd.

When we follow the Good Shepherd, it is behavioral therapy. "... relationships on the brink of failure revealed that relationships don't fail because of *chemistry;* they fail because of *behavior.* Those who regain and deepen their friendship or intimacy succeed by changing how they treat their friends and loved ones."[28]

God has built or recreated us into a New Creation, which requires a "key Acknowledgement" in order to operate and function. That key, like the key to an automobile, must remain in the ignition in order for the Creation to operate. Without the key, it just stops functioning. After the Blood, the Word and the Holy Spirit, we must function and Acknowledge God as the key to the New Creation, this new identity.

A quick reminder: Just because you heard God's voice accurately once, doesn't mean you are always doing so. A classic example of a person listening once to God but then ignoring the voice that got him there is Solomon.

Solomon was the wisest man on the earth, but smart in the spirit isn't good enough. You need to be Acknowledging God every step of the way. We are not "home yet"; this life still has a lot of wilderness in it. Solomon still needed to be Acknowledging God and trusting God, and not leaning upon his own 'wisdom' to achieve what only God wanted to achieve.[29] **And remember, he is the one who wrote Proverbs 3:5-6!**

## THE THIRD FIELD: OUR CALLING/DESTINY

*Brothers, I do not consider myself yet to have laid hold of it. But one thing I do: Forgetting what is behind and straining toward what is ahead, I press toward the mark for the prize of the high calling of God in Christ Jesus.* Philippians 3:13-14

---

[28] *Journal of Family Psychology* 12, No. 4 December 1998, p. 543-556
[29] Even though Solomon wrote Proverbs 3:5-6, he didn't always put it into practice.

Destiny and Calling require an assiduous focus and discipline. We live in an age of disruption. Acknowledgement provides a protective suit that allows us "to live and move and have our being."[30]

## STAY ON YOUR ASSIGNMENT

I remember the time that I was visiting the New York Stock Exchange and a reporter for CNBC was standing next to me. Things with the exchange were kind of messy. There were more and more stocks bought and sold on other exchanges, causing the NYSE to lose its market share. Since the Lord had brought me back to the exchange, I thought, He is giving me access to this journalist.

Well, standing next to the reporter, I interpreted my proximity as my cue to put forth an argument as to why the NYSE was the superior venue for securities transactions, and as I began to explain to him the seriousness of the situation; I was then stopped by a friend. This friend was a governor of the exchange at the time. He said to me, "Tony, just fight the battles God's given you to fight."

"The deadliest seduction leaders face is the wrong-headed focus on solving problems, rather than seizing opportunities," writes Dan Rockwell.[31]

That floor governor's words affected me for years after. I would always view the decision to confront or not to confront an issue from God's perspective and specific assignments: was this my battle or was it someone else's?

Lesson learned: fight the right fights; grow your own garden.

There is an interesting thing about a calling: when the Lord calls you to something, His verb tense is a bit different than ours.

*"(as it is written, 'I have made you a father of many nations') in the presence of Him whom he believed—God, who gives life to the dead and calls those things which do not exist as though they did."* Romans 4:17 **NKJV**

---

30 Acts 17:28
31 Dan Rockwell, Leadership Freak blog

For me it was over 30 years ago when I was sitting at my kitchen table telling God that I would go to work for the department of sanitation, since we had a lot of sanitation workers in our congregation at the time (or so it seemed). Then I blurted out, "But I would like to be a writer."

For the first time in my life I heard this voice inside of me say clearly, "You ARE a writer."

I have to be honest now. I was a little frustrated with all this 'faith stuff.' It struck me as being a little over the top, if you know what I mean. So I said to Him, "If I am a writer, I am going to open my Bible, and I am going to put my finger on a verse. If that verse doesn't confirm what You just said, I will not believe I heard You correctly."

I flipped open my Thompson Chain Reference Bible, and as some may know, it is a voluminous edition with more footnotes than a caterpillar.

There are 31,102 verses in the Bible, and in one way, I was sure that God was going to have His hands full granting the specificity of my request.

I plopped down my right index finger, and under it was this verse in this tiny little book in the Old Testament from Habakkuk 2:2, *"And the LORD answered me, and said,* **Write the vision**, *and make [it] plain upon tables, that he may run that readeth it."*

So realize that when God calls you to something, it is much bigger than your ability to achieve it; it also represents the result of a process that typically takes decades.

Writing out your vision has the effect of cementing the vision.

Right now: If you have been given a vision from the Lord, write it here, right now. If you haven't received your vision or call, that's not a problem. Ask Him, Acknowledge Him and start listening. God's better than FedEx; He knows how to deliver.

## THE FOURTH FIELD: OUR TALENTS AND GIFTS

The lie: Our Talents and Gifts are our pathway to our destiny.

The reality: Talents and Gifts often become life's shiny objects.

Being gifted does not make you immune to the world, the flesh and the devil. In fact, it may make you even more of a target.

## SHINY OBJECT SYNDROME

"The problem is it's easy to get distracted from the goals and commitments you've already made. Rather than seeing things through to completion, you abandon the goals and projects you've already started to chase after whatever new thing has just caught your eye."[32]

Whitney Houston, one of the great singers of this generation, had a talent; but she also had a weakness: strength in one area doesn't eliminate weakness in other areas. Both must be monitored and managed under the unction of the Holy Spirit. We must cultivate our relational life with Christ in concert while yielding to the self-control through the Spirit in the areas of our weaknesses, if we are going to enter into the destiny He has for us.

## RESISTING THE SEDUCTION OF BUSY

*"But Martha was distracted by her many tasks, and she came up and asked, 'Lord, don't You care that my sister has left me to serve alone? So tell her to give me a hand.'"* Luke 10:40

One of the effects of the digital age is the addiction to the busy. Even God-given gifts and talents can become self-defeating mechanisms. With the 5 Fields of Acknowledgement, and with the assistance of the Holy Spirit, our spiritual Systems Analyst (see chapter 2), we are training our hearts and heads to discern the difference between what is important and what is a distraction.

## THE FIELDS OF OUR GIFTS AND TALENTS

Our gifts and talents are intended to do two things: first, point to God and second, have kingdom results. What is a kingdom result? Simply, a kingdom result is anything that establishes righteousness, peace and joy in the Holy Ghost. Note that it is Holy Ghost joy, not the joy of the world, or

---

32 Jack Canfield, http://jackcanfield.com/beat-the-qshiny-objectq-syndrome/

of success or of athletic victory. Joy is the spiritual strength given to us by God in order to withstand adversity or resistance[33] when pursuing God[34] and His purposes.[35]

Matthew 5:16 says it best: *"In the same way, let your light shine before people, so that they can see your good deeds and give honor to your Father in heaven."* [Net Bible]

As long as our gifts are producing light, and causing people to honor our Father, they go beyond being shiny objects; they become signposts and roadmaps.

## THE FIFTH FIELD: ACKNOWLEDGING OUR COMMUNITY

*And when the day of Pentecost was fully come, they were all with one accord in one place. And suddenly there came a sound from heaven as of a rushing mighty wind, and it filled all the house where they were sitting.* Acts 2:1-2

Community is a spiritual phalanx, a group of individuals united for a common purpose.

God has called us through Christ, for a purpose and **with a people**, with whom we share a process. However, certain aspects of our personalities militate against turning to community. We are primarily individuals and we tend to shun community, especially when we are in pain. We may want to throw a pity party for ourselves and invite our friends, but we tend to avoid making the hard decisions and taking the difficult steps that result in true change.

"That's why when it comes to personal change, we first think of our own lack of motivation. Our primary problem isn't that we're weak; it's

---

[33] *For there is a law, for when I would do good, evil is present with me.* Romans 7:21

[34] *After Jesus was born in Bethlehem of Judea in the days of King Herod, wise men from the east arrived unexpectedly in Jerusalem, saying, "Where is He who has been born King of the Jews? For we saw His star in the east and have come to worship Him."* Matthew 2:1-2

[35] *And being warned in a dream not to go back to Herod, they returned to their own country by another route* Matthew 2:12

that we're blind – and when it comes to long-standing habits, what you can't see is usually what's controlling you."[36]

Community often acts as a backup system or redundancy system that confirms our original callings.

*"Wherefore I put thee in remembrance that thou stir up the gift of God, which is in thee by the putting on of my hands."* 2 Timothy 1:6

Spiritual community under the influence of the Holy Spirit is not only an extra pair of eyes to protect against blindness, but it is within community that our gifting and calling will be fully realized. Paul was not just anointed and sent out as an apostle. Paul was mentored and discipled by Barnabas, and then over a course of time Paul and Barnabas were commissioned to go on missions by their spiritual community.

Our spiritual communities commission us as well and provide us enormous resources that we don't possess personally. Christianity was never meant to be a solo act. A community is almost like the supply line that delivers all the supplies and munitions necessary to conduct the warfare. Where you lack something, the community many times can provide it.[37]

Community has always been vulnerable to attack. Envy, jealousy, ambition, competition creep into the 'camp.' We can see it started back in Genesis 4, when Cain became jealous of Abel because Abel's sacrifice was acceptable. We can even see it with Esau and Jacob, where Jacob desired the birthright of the firstborn, and cheated Esau out of it. Then we see when Jacob had his 12 sons, they conspired and sold Joseph into slavery, because of Jacob's favoritism of Joseph. I believe that community is something we must be vigilant to preserve and protect.

---

36 *Change Anything*, p. 9 by Kerry Patterson, Joseph Grenny, David Maxfield
37 In another way also, community, when it is not functioning, can become a liability. Today's urban gangs are examples of what a toxic community does. Gangs provide an identity, 'fellowship' and even protection, but at what price?

## *Chapter 10*

# ACKNOWLEDGEMENT IS CONFIRMED AND AFFIRMED IN COMMUNITY

## 7 BENEFITS OF COMMUNITY

1. Community is the environment in which dignity is a core value
2. Community is a source of empowerment and confidence
3. Community provides a launchpad and incubator for vision and calling
4. Community is the classroom for life's adult education
5. Community provides a basecamp from which we engage in spiritual warfare
6. Community provides us spiritual covering
7. Community offers us accountability

As stated earlier, I believe God has called us through Christ, for a purpose and with a people with whom we share a process. Community is God's pattern of the Kingdom. All the great moves of God called for a spiritual unity that created an invisible force that forged the collective and individual destinies of a people.

Remember that the Hebrews left Egypt as a group; the Israelites entered Canaan as a group; and the church received the baptism of the Holy Spirit as a group.

## COMMUNITY RELEASES THE HOLY SPIRIT

The Scripture from Acts 2 is worth reiterating:

*And when the day of Pentecost was fully come, they were all with one accord in one place. And suddenly there came a sound from heaven as of a rushing mighty wind, and it filled all the house where they were sitting.* Acts 2:1

It uses the word accord, which indicates that they were in agreement in mind, in purpose and in heart. The Greek word for accord is not used until the arrival of the Holy Spirit in Acts (it is not even used in the Gospels).

## ONE. COMMUNITY IS AN ENVIRONMENT IN WHICH DIGNITY IS A CORE VALUE

This dignity is also referred to today as a safe place. Maybe we have gotten too used to sitting in pews, and then we get divided into two groups of people, 'the sitters' and 'the standers.' The standers are in control of what happens in and at a meeting (or so they think). The sitters are the audience that financially supports the standers in their standing. Standers are also called other things: clergy, leaders and ministers. Sitters are laity, people, congregates, donors, and they usually maintain their respective positions.

Christianity in North America has morphed into Sit-Yanity; we are sitters. Not babysitters, pew sitters. When the Israelites entered the Promised Land, there was no sitting. All productive lives had to be taking their own ground as a group: the only other time when they weren't moving forward was when they had to put it into 'reverse gear,' also known as repentance.

Dignity with God isn't based upon who we are, but rather who He is making us; and the benchmark is always based on who He is. One good thing about God is that He knows what He's doing. Hopefully, as the community functions properly, we come into direct vital communication with God's real purposes, His perspective for our lives and in spiritual communication with each other and the world.

### TWO. COMMUNITY IS A SOURCE OF EMPOWERMENT AND CONFIDENCE

The by-product of community is personal and individual clarity. If you are eating at the table, you have a say at the table.

There is a TV show I like to watch, *Blue Bloods*, and in each episode there is always a scene in which 4 generations are sitting at the table. Each person has a seat, and each person is entitled to have a say. The father, of course, has a final say, but the education that emerges from the conversation is always one that empowers individuals to think and see outside of his or her own box.

It is during the meal that each one of the family members has an opportunity to Acknowledge each other and who they are with respect to their position in the family. They even learn how to sow seeds of Acknowledgement into each other's lives so that they become empowered people.

### THREE. COMMUNITY IS A LAUNCHPAD AND INCUBATOR FOR VISION AND CALLING

After food, clothing, shelter and identity, what a community or family provides is direction, purpose and vision.

Direction derives from calling; purpose is integrated with his or her talents and gifts; and vision is attached to who they are as well as the legacy they are called to leave. All vision is born in prayer, and in our prayer time is when we take time to Acknowledge God, Ourselves, Callings, Destiny and Community. Prayers of Acknowledgement get God involved in everything at the outset, rather than getting Him in to do the clean-up after we have made a mistake or two.

## FOUR. COMMUNITY IS THE CLASSROOM FOR LIFE'S ADULT EDUCATION

Community provides not only a base but also guidelines under which we are to function. Here is where the "shall not's" and the "shalls" become very valuable. Shall not: murder, covet your neighbor's wife, servant or goods, and shall not lie and gossip about your neighbor. It is also the context by which we learn to love our neighbor.

## FIVE. COMMUNITY PROVIDES A BASECAMP FROM WHICH WE ENGAGE IN SPIRITUAL WARFARE

Community through Acknowledgement not only changes atmospheres, but it opens the doors to miracles. Often those miracles distill down to each person based upon their specific calling and assignment. But never forget that the purpose of community in the Kingdom is **not** to produce a culture of complacency, but rather community and warfare go together. **If you are not taking ground, you are losing it from a Kingdom perspective.**

## SIX. COMMUNITY PROVIDES US SPIRITUAL COVERING

Paul and Barnabas functioned in concert with the prayers and covering of their local church. And in Paul's case, he maintained a clear channel of communication with those churches he planted through his journeys, imprisonments and epistles. Were it not for those letters, the church as we know it today would be completely different.

The community's spiritual covering does so much more than just provide a babysitting service but also a buffer and safe place in the storms.

## SEVEN. COMMUNITY OFFERS US ACCOUNTABILITY

The spiritual community also will reveal to us the new vistas that God is pioneering in each generation. An example of this is the 3,000-year-old tradition, circumcision, which was discontinued in the light of the new covenant which produced a 'circumcision of the heart.' (Romans 2:29) It was within community that a powerful tradition and rite was abandoned for a circumcision of the heart. All of this could not have occurred without the existence of community.

## CIRCUMCISION

We were almost Jews if it weren't for Paul and James, the brother of Jesus!!

Back in the early church days, circumcision was the biggest distinguishing feature that set apart the Jews from all other religions and faiths. Not only was it severe, but it was something that was the first ritual given to the descendants of Abraham representing the original covenant with God:

*This is my covenant, which ye shall keep, between me and you and thy seed after thee; Every man child among you shall be circumcised.* Genesis 17:10

So when Paul left Antioch and traveled to Jerusalem to discuss his mission to the Gentiles with Peter and the other apostles, circumcision had to be brought up. In the Book of Acts, Paul says, *"They recognized that I had been entrusted with the good news for the un-circumcised."* The Acts of the Apostles describes the dispute as being resolved by Peter's speech and concluding with a decision by James, the brother of Jesus, not to require circumcision from Gentile converts. Acts quotes Peter and James as saying:

*"My brothers, you are well aware that from early days God made his choice among you that through my mouth the Gentiles would hear the word of the gospel and believe. And God, who knows the heart, bore witness by granting them the Holy Spirit just as he did us. He made no distinction between us and them, for by faith he purified their hearts. Why, then, are you now putting God to the test by placing on the shoulders of the disciples a yoke that neither our ancestors nor we have been able to bear? On the contrary, we believe that we are saved through the grace of the Lord Jesus, in the same way as they."* Acts 15:7–11

When James confirmed what Paul was admonishing the apostles to do, it would be carried out through the community, and preserved through the centuries thereafter. It was a very big decision to reverse a tradition held for 3,000 years, but very necessary, considering the significance of Calvary and the Resurrection of Jesus.

## IN REVIEW

* Individuals and spiritual communities need to 'cultivate' the agrarian mindset that once guided their relational model with God.
* There needs to be a rediscovery of the process and principles that govern the laws of sowing and reaping and incorporating them into our Christian walk.
* Our Christian faith calls for a tangible and ongoing relationship with God by discerning and responding to His voice.
* Our relationship with God isn't based upon ritual but upon developing a relationship to God as a Father, Jesus as Savior and Spirit as Teacher.
* We must learn to segment and integrate each of the 5 spiritual fields of faith we are called to maintain: God, ourselves, our destiny, our gifts and talents, and our communities.

As a final way to emphasize how vital this concept of fields is, the following was found in an Iowa newspaper,[38] which centered on a group of farmers who had recently begun to conduct prayer services for the blessing of their fields. According to the piece, the farmers from Riceville understand they are graced with some of the richest soil in the world, and consequently, they are responsible to cultivate this ground.

In recognition of this stewardship, they would gather together, "…to pray standing among seeds waiting to be planted, to pray for blessings on their fields in this planting season."

---

38 http://globegazette.com/news/local/farmers-pray-for-blessings-on-their-fields/article_0984e060-9671-5c1c-9f47-4943b5e89be2.html

The article went on to describe about how for seven springs the Riceville Ministerial Association has held such a blessing of the fields in the town. The blessing tradition began with a wedding in one of the fields, and then to people starting to hold church in that field and now they hold a blessing service for the seeds, fields and harvest. (They also hold a separate service before Labor Day, preceding the harvest.)

One of the pastors involved even referred to the soils as Iowa's black gold (with over 450 soil types in Iowa, that's a lot of gold). The secular paper's article didn't shy away from covering the thinking behind such a community. It stated:

"Farmers spend many hours evaluating their type of soil and planning for each upcoming planting season, but no matter how much they do; there is no guarantee of a crop. Success has nothing to do with us. It comes from God alone," said Pastor Scott Meyer.

"It is by the grace of God that the seeds grow and another harvest is realized. He finds it in His love to bless us with a bountiful crop."

He reminded everyone that each person is a different type of soil "that needs something different to lead each of us into the Christian life."

"Just like each farmer evaluates what nutrients are needed for his crops, we also need spiritual food to become good soil for our Christian lives," said Meyer. "May God bless our fields to feed his people and God bless us in the spirit of the Christian community."

Pastor Dan Christensen said, "After attending a service like this, I hope people are a little more aware that God is in control of our lives. No matter where we are, whether it is in the field or where we work, we are in the hands of God."

To me this profoundly symbolizes the power and resilience of the Acknowledged Life in action.

## PRAYER OF ACKNOWLEDGEMENT

Lord, this day I Acknowledge You first of all: in the Cross, the Spirit and the Word.

I also Acknowledge You in all my ways and life: my calling, abilities, opportunities, communities, especially in all my covenant relationships: marriage, family, friendships, work, community, and church.

I Acknowledge I was born, redeemed, transformed and assigned to be an expression of Your wisdom, mercy and justice to this generation.

Kingdom, let it come; Your will, let it be done today.

## Chapter 11

# ACKNOWLEDGEMENTS & MINDSETS

## ACKNOWLEDGEMENT

Lord, at times when there is fog, I trust and Acknowledge that You will direct my steps, even if the fog is the result of what I have done. This Acknowledgement is my fog horn to You.

## KEY POINTS

* Acknowledgement empowers me to pull down and cast down the imaginations that oppose obedience and submission to You.
* Acknowledgement has quickened me; I am ready because you have prepared the victory dinner for me.
* I Acknowledge that my conversations with You feed me with the faith that is fierce. The Acknowledged Life is a mental approach whereby I engage God's purposes, timing and assignments. Acknowledgement is not when I take my work and attach a "God" label to it.

Acknowledgement is our intentional, active engagement of God in the context of our present state.

The Acknowledged Life possesses an Acknowledged Mind, which is **all-whether thinking.** Whether this happens or that happens, the Acknowledged Mind adjusts based upon the characteristics of the Christian walk as outlined in Ephesians chapter one.[39]

When I Acknowledge God, I adopt an attitude I believe to be consist with the purposes of God in the present season. Different mindsets are predicated on different seasons: like the decision to wear a short-sleeved shirt in July.

## MINDSETS

**Definition of Mindset**: A mindset is the lens through which we see and interpret where we are and consequently where we need to be.

Another equally enlightening description of what a mindset is comes from Wikipedia: "A mindset is a set of **assumptions**, **methods**, or notations held by one or more people or groups of people that is so **established** that it creates a powerful incentive within these people or groups to continue **to adopt or accept prior behaviors, choices**, or tools. This phenomenon is also sometimes described as **mental inertia, 'groupthink,' or a 'paradigm,'** and it is often difficult to counteract its effects upon analysis and decision making processes."[40]

Mindsets can change, depending upon the longevity and the pressure being exerted upon the individual to change. The word for 'conformed' [Gr. Syschēmatizō[41]] in Romans 12:2 "...*be not conformed to this world...*" is comprised of two parts: *syn*, meaning with and *schema*, meaning the habitus,[42] as comprising everything in a person including the senses, the figure, bearing, discourse, actions, manner of life.

We must be intentional about our mindsets.

"*Let this mind be in you, which was also in Christ Jesus*" Phil 2:5

---

39 Blessed, Chosen, Predestined, Accepted, Redeemed, Abounding, Known Inheritor, Sealed
40 https://en.wikipedia.org/wiki/Mindset
41 Syschēmatizō: to conform one's self (i.e., one's mind and character) to another's pattern
42 The word habitus is the word from which we draw our word habit.

Mindsets are the starting point of a dynamic progression that proceeds as follows:

Mindsets determine Alignment,
Alignment determines Actions,
Actions determine Outcome,
Outcome manifests Source.

The importance of how our outcomes manifest the source is that it will either point men to us or point men to the Lord. *"Let your light so shine before men, that they may see your good works, and glorify your Father which is in heaven."*[43]

## THE ACKNOWLEDGED MIND

The Acknowledged Life reflects a proactive mind – proactive in that it is being activated and led by the Holy Spirit. Such a mind understands the power and value in stopping to Acknowledge the Lord in every area, like a GPS system that adjusts based upon location. The Acknowledging suspends our thoughts, feelings and understanding[44] in order to yield to the Lord, in the event we miss an exit or turn.

Our thoughts are the things that we 'put on' even before we get dressed and walk out the door.

As a parent, you can remember countless times you had tried to dress your child, but the child wouldn't stop moving around until you 'arrested' their activity by saying: "I can't get you dressed if you won't stop moving! **Stand still!**"

Our Acknowledgements stop us from 'moving around' **and reminds us to stand still**. Prayer allows us to dress our minds so that we may be able to dress for the kind of spiritual weather we will encounter that day.

---

43  Matthew 5:16

44  Proverbs 3:5 Trust in the Lord with all your heart and **lean not unto your own understanding.**

## MINDSETS ARE THE FRUIT OF CONVERSATIONS

Predicated upon our prior "conversations" that produce our beliefs, we take action and live our lives in agreement and alignment with our 'belief grid.' Belief is not only what we ascertain to be the present condition, but it also projects what we expect to occur in the future. Some of those projections, as we see on Wall Street every day, are wrong.

Back in the Garden, Adam and Eve had a conversation with God where they learned they were free to eat of any tree in the garden except the tree of the knowledge of good and evil that grew in the *"midst of the garden."* Eating of the fruit of that tree would lead to their deaths.

When Eve thoughtlessly engaged in a conversation with the serpent, little did she realize this conversation would ultimately cause the actions that would separate her from God and Adam.

Gen 3:1 *"Now the serpent was craftier than any other beast of the field that the LORD God had made. He said to the woman, "Did God actually say, 'You shall not eat of any tree in the garden'?" 2 And the woman said to the serpent, "We may eat of the fruit of the trees in the garden, 3 but God said, 'You shall not eat of the fruit of the tree that is in the midst of the garden, neither shall you touch it, lest you die.'" 4 But the serpent said to the woman, "You will not surely die. 5 For God knows that when you eat of it your eyes will be opened, and you will be like God, knowing good and evil." 6 So when the woman saw that the tree was good for food, and that it was a delight to the eyes, and that the tree was to be desired to make one wise, she took of its fruit and ate, and she also gave some to her husband who was with her, and he ate. 7 Then the eyes of both were opened, and they knew that they were naked. And they sewed fig leaves together and made themselves loincloths."*

## EVE'S CONVERSATION WITH THE SERPENT DEMONSTRATED 4 THINGS:

She wasn't seeing what God was seeing
She didn't see the problem with disobeying God

She didn't see that she was conspiring with Satan
She didn't see the truth of what the Lord told her about the tree

Eve was **in** the Garden, and she still didn't **see it**. What does that say to us?

For Eve, and for many of us, although she was in a Garden, her heart and head were in a desert.

**The conversation Eve had with the serpent produced a mindset of distrust, discouragement, fear and confusion.** Her actions led to outcomes – outcomes that would have an impact on all who came after her. One outcome is that man was now subject to disease and death, as predicted by God.

God's first action of recourse was to clothe Adam and Eve with animal skins instead of their leafy manufactured coverings.

There is a great deal of significance in both the idea that God clothed them and that the leaves they put together weren't good enough. It would take a sacrifice and shedding the blood of an innocent to cover them and that sacrifice would ultimately foreshadow the word and the revealed mind of Christ.

## RENEWED MINDSETS

Mindsets are aligned either Godward or manward. Eve allowed the serpent to realign her mindset from being Godward to manward. When our mindsets are manward they frequently involve a filter: fear, especially fear of lack. Consequently, the mindset must be renewed on a daily, even on a moment-to-moment basis (Romans 12:1-2). This renewal then realigns us back toward God. God instructs us to implement this renewal lifestyle, which calls for a two-step process:

First, through the Acknowledged Life, we must "put off" any sin (any hurt, unforgiveness, doubt, fear, rebellion, self-centeredness, lust, bitterness, etc.), any corrupt thinking, or any barrier that would quench God's Spirit and "put on" the Mind of Christ (2 Corinthians 10:5).

Renewing our minds is not simply "changing" our thoughts, but actually putting off the old, negative thoughts as well as putting on God's Thoughts. In other words, we can't just say to God, "Lord, give me Your Thoughts," and somehow expect Him to "automatically" give us His Mind. We must first put off our own self-centered thinking by confessing, repenting, and then giving it to God.

Second, at this point, we can then put on the "Mind of Christ."[45] When we put on the Mind of Christ, we are actually tuning into heaven's conversation. You see, an Acknowledged Life not only is thinking God's Thoughts but it is **making way for God's Acts**! This is what the early church did. What started in the Upper Room consequently produced the 5th book of the New Testament, called Acts. It is not ACTSident!! LOL

## ALIGNMENT

The degree that our mindset is aligned with heaven will determine how far our faith will take us. When David came upon Goliath for the first time, his reaction to him wasn't, "Holy smoke! No wonder you guys are quaking in your armor. This dude is MASSIVE!!"

No. David said, *"…for who is this uncircumcised Philistine, that he should defy the armies of the living God?"*[46]

You see, David's mindset was not only of a shepherd, but that of a believer, who spent a great deal of his time worshiping God. And it wasn't just the God of his fathers, or of Moses, it was *"…the living God."* His psalms were the evidence of the depths of his God-encounters.[47]

By the time David arrived with lunch for his brothers and witnessed the champion Goliath, he was ready. David didn't have to raise his game.

---

45 Nancy Missler https://www.khouse.org/articles/2015/1237/print/
46 1 Samuel 17:26
47 If prayer is the by-product of our conversation with God, David's psalms represent a musical duet inspired by the Holy Spirit. That is why it is so easy to pray the Psalms, because they are simply prayers sung with and to God.

David's game was already raised because his mindset was aligned with the mind of God.

Until those days when they were facing off against the Philistines and their giant, Israel was accustomed to God doing victory for them:

> Moses' rod touching the Red Sea and the Hebrews walking through on dry land
> Moses bringing them through the wilderness
> Joshua seeing the walls of Jericho fall down with a trumpet blast

It was almost like they were facing the Philistines saying, "OK, God, we are here. Let's go! Do something! Will you?"

It took a David, a shepherd,[48] to show Israel their God wanted to take them to go to the next spiritual level.

<u>Israel's mindset</u> was in alignment with the Moses-Joshua model, which was waiting for God to do something; David's mindset[49] was aligned with God's new playbook (the New Testament), and what He was now empowering David to do.

The actions of Saul and the army – to run away from the giant – were the result of the mindset **limited by their past victories**. David's actions – to charge headlong toward the giant intent on his destruction – was the result of his mindset of God and David's **future exploits.**

That's why he could not use Saul's armor. Saul's armor would only encumber David, using an armor that made no room for the breastplate of righteousness. In his hands, a sling became the sword of the Spirit.

One mindset was holding them back; the other would ultimately set them free and give them victory.

---

[48] Again, the Lord occupationally positions another shepherd as His leadership paradigm for a Christian leader. This is a juxtaposition with the secular model, which places a leader on a platform instead of a pasture. A shepherd leads, feeds, guards and guides. A leader doesn't dictate.

[49] Leadership calls for the leader to go before the army. Jesus tells the disciples in John 14:2, I go to prepare a place for you.

David's actions on the battlefront were the result of his Godward alignment. When David was with the sheep, he never stopped Acknowledging God even when he was alone 'behind the lines.'

### WINESKINS → MINDSKINS

Through the gospels and New Testament, it is an excursion into a new territory – the world and mind of God's spirit and kingdom.

Our mindsets are meant to contain the fruit and the manna of God's kingdom: His wisdom, His joy, and His peace. Acknowledgement points us toward, plugs us into and allows us to be partakers of the realities of God.

One of the ways Jesus taught about this new mental model was by comparing mindsets to wineskins.

*And no one puts new wine into old wineskins. If he does, the new wine will burst the skins and it will be spilled, and the skins will be destroyed. 38 But new wine must be put into fresh wineskins. 39 And no one after drinking old wine desires new, for he says, 'The old is good.'* Luke 5:37-38 ESV

This passage contains at least 4 points that Jesus looks to communicate to His disciples:

> **First:** With each growing season comes a new vintage. Seasons of new spiritual growth always produce new joy and new victory.
> **Second:** The crushed juices of the fruit (grapes) are contained in wineskins, not grape skins. This parallelism is not coincidental. The skins of fruit can't contain the juices that they produce. They are only contained in animal skins, requiring the death of that animal, AKA: sacrifice. Consequently, sacrifice is necessary to contain the new wine.
> **Third:** Every growing season will call for its own sacrifice to preserve the crop for harvest.
> **Fourth:** People who drink the wine of one season are reticent to taste the wine of seasons that follow; believing the wine of the new season could not match or even exceed that of the old vintage.

## *Chapter 12*

# 5 MINDSETS | 5 WINESKINS

## ACKNOWLEDGEMENT

Acknowledging God keeps you in correct spiritual alignment with heaven.

## KEY POINT

* Acknowledgement also places you in direct opposition to Satan.

It is critical that our spiritual wineskins – let's call them "mindskins" – validate and build upon scripture, just as the New Covenant validates and builds upon the Old Testament. Our mindskin – our thinking and actions – will either yield fruit or failure, depending on whether or not our wineskin contains the fruit that God is producing.

In some ways, a mindskin is the map by which we expect to navigate over the course of our day and our lives. It is comprised of information (see chapter 2) filtered through our beliefs. As long as that belief-tempered information flows, it enables us to function using what Paul refers to as the mind of Christ.

Thus the mindskin is the cognitive structure through which we filter and function information based upon the revealed knowledge which we believe is governing the context.

## CHARACTERISTICS OF MINDSKINS

What I have learned, especially as a result of studying the scriptures, is that mindskins have the following characteristics:

> **Mindskins can become outdated** – with the birth of Christ, the Old Covenant would ultimately become outdated and yield to the New Covenant. Even though the spiritual mindskins were for the most part proven and true, when God does a new thing, the mindskin will have to change. Old mindskins can't contain the new wine of fresh revelation.
>
> **Mindskins are intrinsically resistant to change** – what we become familiar with becomes a behavior that we view as an asset rather than a liability. People can become very stubborn and be attached to their mindskin because of the risk attached to venturing into something they don't know. This resistance is because people are comfortable with their old approaches. A new revelation will require the sacrifice necessary to contain the new wine and thereby the new mindskin.
>
> **Mindskins are susceptible to confirming our old paradigms** – an old mindskin is convenient, especially to people who are too busy to consider other options. Our mindskins are the benchmark by which we assess, value and make choices.
>
> **Mindskins are incomplete** – and as much as we believe what we know is all there is, it is still incomplete. We are seeing through a glass darkly.

*For now we see through a glass, darkly; but then face to face: now I know in part; but then shall I know even as also I am known.* 1 Corinthians 13:12

I believe there are primarily 5 kinds of mindskins:

**False:** fraudulent mindskin
**Old:** traditional mindskin
**Irrational:** emotional mindskin
**Erroneous:** flawed or naïve mindskin
**New:** new mindskin
**False Mindskin:** A Fraudulent Mindskin

Fraudulent mindskins are based upon a falsehood, and that falsehood is usually traced back to a deception, whether we are a victim or a perpetrator.

## BEING DECEIVED

In Genesis 3 regarding Eve and the serpent, God said, *"Do not eat or you will die."* The serpent said, *"You will not surely die."* Eve's conversation with the serpent, in which he deceived her, blinded her to the goodness of God, and that produced despair, and despair yielded a harvest of death through disobedience.

## BEING A DECEIVER

Sometimes a mindskin is fraudulent because we are trying to deceive, either others or ourselves. Usually these deceptions are designed to protect us or our vested interests.

Jesus challenged the Pharisees, in dramatic fashion, and their deception over how they had turned the temple into their private piggybank.

*12 And Jesus went into the temple of God, and cast out all them that sold and bought in the temple, and overthrew the tables of the moneychangers, and the seats of them that sold doves,*

*13 And said unto them, It is written, My house shall be called the house of prayer; but ye have made it a den of thieves.* Mt 21:12 [similarly in Mark 11:15 and John 2:14]

The religious leadership had co-opted God's command to take sacrifices to the temple by acting as the religious 'brokers' between the people and the acts of sacrifice, perpetrating this racket in the temple and making money off of the whole process.

Jesus exposed this false mindskin. He not only decried the money-changing, but displayed how He felt about the sanctity of God's house in the process. While not every false mindskin will incur such a reaction from Our Lord, we cannot operate in His power and authority through deception.

**Old Mindskin:** Traditions

Jesus knew the apostles would have a bit of a 'transition' period following the resurrection. They had developed the habit of physically following Jesus and going where He sent them. They had a physical guide for over 3 years; they saw where He went and they came along. Now He was gone. What do we do?

With the absence of their physical guide, Jesus, the apostles fell back on their traditions. Traditions often substitute as the 'guide' by which we are 'led' in faith, even when that leading takes us into a spiritual cul-de-sac. It can require an encounter with God to get us back on the path.

One example is found in Acts chapter 10, with Cornelius and Peter. Cornelius, we read, was *"A centurion of what was known as the Italian Cohort, a devout man who feared God with all his household, gave alms generously to the people, and prayed continually to God."* An angel tells Cornelius, *"Your prayers and your alms have ascended as a memorial before God. 5 And now send men to Joppa and bring one Simon who is called Peter."* Acts 10:1-2, 5

So we see here a Gentile, Cornelius, a leader of Roman soldiers, characterized as one who is continually praying to a God he does not know and, in addition to his prayers, he is a giver. God is moved.

Meanwhile, back in Joppa, Peter is up on a housetop praying and he falls into a trance. The Holy Spirit gives him a vision where he:

*"...saw the heavens opened and something like a great sheet descending, being let down by its four corners upon the earth. 12 In it were all kinds of animals and*

*reptiles and birds of the air. 13 And there came a voice to him: "Rise, Peter; kill and eat." 14 But Peter said, "By no means, Lord; for I have never eaten anything that is common or unclean." 15 And the voice came to him again a second time, "What God has made clean, do not call common." 16 This happened three times, and the thing was taken up at once to heaven.* Acts 10:11-16

Peter is then summoned to Cornelius's home. He goes, with some of the "brothers." When he meets Cornelius, Peter says, *"You yourselves know how unlawful it is for a Jew to associate with or to visit anyone of another nation, but God has shown me that I should not call any person common or unclean. 29 So when I was sent for, I came without objection."* Acts 10:28-29

Peter then shares the gospel with all present and God moves:

*While Peter was still saying these things, the Holy Spirit fell on all who heard the word. 45 And the believers from among the circumcised who had come with Peter were amazed, because the gift of the Holy Spirit was poured out even on the Gentiles. 46 For they were hearing them speaking in tongues and extolling God. Then Peter declared, 47 "Can anyone withhold water for baptizing these people, who have received the Holy Spirit just as we have?"* Acts 10:44-47

In the Acknowledged Life, there is a distinction between a tradition and a process. A tradition is a spiritual 'formula' that is implemented to achieve a kingdom outcome. However, by blindly following the rules, we can end up boxing-out God. There is no engagement, just execution. But a process is a transformational journey that begins with an encounter (the Holy Spirit showing Peter the vision of different food), requiring an engagement (Peter accepting this new revelation and understanding its larger context) and leading to a distinct outcome (the salvation of Cornelius and his family, and the realization that Jesus is savior of Gentiles, as well as Jews).

But let's not forget, every tradition began as a revelation. Peter stood at a crossroad where he was forced to adjust his thinking to accomplish a broader mission.

So in learning from Peter, we that adhere to tradition should not blind ourselves from missing the next move of God. Remember Jesus telling them about how their approach to the law was disempowering:

*"Making the word of God of none effect through your tradition, which ye have delivered."* Mark 7:13 ESV

The practice of using traditions as a substitute for the active word of God is by no means limited to the first-century Christians. Prior to the 1960s, it was considered heretical to use a guitar in a worship service. Organs and pianos were the only instruments recognized as appropriate for worship – perhaps an orchestra or certain classical ensembles. Then the culture changed and musical tastes changed, and back in the mid-sixties the Catholic Church permitted folk Masses, where guitars and even drums were used to accompany songs of worship, a phenomenon that continues to this day. Somehow those 'unclean' instruments became clean.

**Irrational | Emotional Mindskin:** Bias and Bigotry

In Paul's case, he was persecuting Christians, even having them killed because he was convinced they were a heretical splinter group that was damaging the Jewish people. Paul knew the scriptures inside and out. His theology was flawless, and yet his theology brought him into direct conflict with the Holy Spirit.

Acts 8:1-3 *And Saul approved of his execution [Stephen's]. And there arose on that day a great persecution against the church in Jerusalem, and they were all scattered throughout the regions of Judea and Samaria, except the apostles. Devout men buried Stephen and made great lamentation over him. But Saul was ravaging the church, and entering house after house, he dragged off men and women and committed them to prison.*

**Erroneous Mindskin:** Flawed

In the Book of Acts we read the Gentiles were being adopted into this new move of God, including receiving the baptism of the Holy Spirit. Until that point, only the Jews were the recipients of such a manifestation, and considering the thousands of years the Lord had concentrated on the preservation of this one people, it contradicted not only their law but their sense of their exclusivity in God's sight. You were either a Jew or a Gentile; you were either in or out.

Paul has a profound revelation on the road to Damascus [Acts 9] that forces him to change his mindskin about who Jesus is and how He was calling Paul – formerly Saul – to minister to many, including the Gentiles. After his conversion, Paul begins preaching the gospel to all who would listen. He confronts Peter in Antioch stating that the Gospel is for everyone not based upon the Jewish tradition of circumcision or even on the law. In his letter to the church in Galatia he writes,

*We ourselves are Jews by birth and not Gentile sinners; yet we know that a person is not justified by works of the law but through faith in Jesus Christ, so we also have believed in Christ Jesus, in order to be justified by faith in Christ and not by works of the law, because by works of the law no one will be justified.* Galatians 2:15-16 ESV

Even when he was Saul, persecutor of Christians, Jesus acknowledged him as His minister to Gentiles and changed his name to Paul and his destiny to one of tireless service to the Lord. And this Paul, as a result of his new mindskin, is still impacting us to this day.

**New Mindskin:** Renewed and Revealed

There are two examples worth examining from scripture of individuals who Acknowledge God and embrace a new mindskin. The first is Nicodemus.

Nicodemus ben Gorion, the brother of the historian Josephus, was a wealthy member of the Sanhedrin, the court of 70 elders, which was the highest religious body of the Jewish community in Jerusalem in Jesus' day. As a Pharisee, Nicodemus was a noted teacher of the Old Testament and, like all learned Jews, traced his lineage to Abraham, upon which his entire religious hope rested. We might say Nicodemus' mindskin was wrapped up in being Abraham's seed.

Jesus encounters him when Nicodemus approaches Jesus at night, away from prying eyes, to engage Jesus in a conversation that is well known to most believers. As recorded in the third chapter of the Gospel of John, Nicodemus begins by establishing Jesus' credentials. *"Rabbi, we know that you are come from God, for no one could do these signs you do unless God is with him."* John 3:2 ESV

Jesus, speaking into Nicodemus' mindskin, gives him new information, *"Jesus answered him truly, truly I say to you, unless one is born again he cannot see the kingdom of God."* v. 3

Nicodemus, in true rabbinic form, explores this comment with a seeking question, *"How can a man be born when he is already old? Can he enter a second time into his mother's womb and be born?"* v. 4

Jesus proceeds to unpack this critical concept to Nicodemus:

*5 Jesus answered, "Truly, truly, I say to you, unless one is born of water and the Spirit, he cannot enter the kingdom of God. 6 That which is born of the flesh is flesh, and that which is born of the Spirit is spirit. 7 Do not marvel that I said to you, 'You must be born again.' 8 The wind blows where it wishes, and you hear its sound, but you do not know where it comes from or where it goes. So it is with everyone who is born of the Spirit."*

Nicodemus is skeptical, *"How can these things be?"* v. 9b

Jesus goes to the heart of the matter:

*[16] "For God so loved the world, that he gave his only Son, that whoever believes in him should not perish but have eternal life. [17] For God did not send his Son into the world to condemn the world, but in order that the world might be saved through him. [18] Whoever believes in him is not condemned, but whoever does not believe is condemned already, because he has not believed in the name of the only Son of God."*

According to *The Encyclopedia of the Bible*,

At a later time Nicodemus defended, even if hesitantly, Jesus before the Sanhedrin, insisting, *"Does our law judge a man without first giving him a hearing and learning what he does?"* (John 7:51). This brought the taunting reply, *"Are you from Galilee too? Search and you will see that no prophet is to arise from Galilee"* (John 7:52). At the time of Jesus' burial he came out into the open and brought spices with which to anoint the body and assisted in the burial (John 19:39-42).[50]

I believe Nicodemus Acknowledged the truth of Jesus and His message. This Acknowledgement caused him to change from his old mindskin – 'I can rely on my identity as Abraham's seed to ensure my destiny with God' – to his new mindskin – 'I'm born again through Jesus.'

It is critical that our mindskins be flexible and able to adapt to new information, ideas and beliefs in order to accommodate the new wine God is pouring forth. Gamaliel, our second example of new mindskins, shows

---

50 https://www.biblegateway.com/resources/encyclopedia-of-the-bible/Nicodemus

this kind of flexibility. Gamaliel was a celebrated Jewish doctor, teacher of the law, Paul's tutor and an advisor to the Sanhedrin.

As such, Gamaliel should have been a staunch supporter of the status quo, an advocate of the position taken by the Sanhedrin that Jesus and His followers were heretics and had to be stamped out. However, when the Sanhedrin arrested Peter and some of the apostles for preaching the gospel with the intention of eradicating them, Gamaliel said, *"So in the present case I tell you, keep away from these men and let them alone, for if this plan or this undertaking is of man, it will fail; but if it is of God, you will not be able to overthrow them. You might even be found opposing God!"* Acts 5:38-39 ESV

**To review:** Our mindsets are the results of our earthly, spiritual and worship conversations (prayer & praise). These 'conversations' help to produce our spiritual wineskins, AKA mindskins.

A mindskin is the result of our acts of sacrifice and obedience to conform to the image of Christ.

There are 5 different kinds of these mindskins (experiential knowledge):

**False:** false mindskin – Eve's thinking which resulted in the Fall
**Old:** traditional mindskin – caused the Pharisees not to recognize Jesus
**Irrational:** emotional mindskin – Paul's decision to persecute the church
**Erroneous:** flawed or naïve mindskin – present day, the Church not renewal
**New:** new mindskin – ability to recognize Jesus as savior

## PRAYER OF ACKNOWLEDGEMENT

Lord, I Acknowledge You today, now, in my life. I take this moment to recognize You. And I pray that what You have done for me in the past will not distract me from what You desire to do in my future.

I ask the Father, in Jesus' name, to give to me spiritual wisdom and insight so that I might grow in the knowledge of God. I pray that my heart will be flooded with Your light so that I can apprehend the hope for this rich and glorious inheritance. I pray also that I would operate in the incredible greatness of the Father's power that He has provided for us as we believe Him — this is the same mighty power that raised Jesus from the dead and seated Him in the place of honor at God's right hand in the heavenly realms. In all these things and for Your purposes I pray in Jesus' name.

## *Chapter 13*

# RELEASING HEAVEN'S ATMOSPHERE

## ACKNOWLEDGEMENT

God, You are so good. You have authorized me to speak out, declare out and transform the atmosphere to release the oxygen of heaven. I breathe You in and I Acknowledge You out into every circumstance.

## KEY POINTS

* Acknowledgement is the ability to activate, prioritize and influence non-productive mindsets and cultures
* Acknowledgement is the safeguard against doubt and fear
* Acknowledgement keeps the conversation of hope going until desire arrives
* Acknowledgement is the trigger on the shotgun of hope

*Every victory begins with a change of atmosphere.*

## ACKNOWLEDGEMENT IS THE MINDSET THAT RELEASES HEAVEN'S ATMOSPHERE

The atmosphere of the Acknowledged mind releases vision, belief, hope and faith. It is through these "spiritual elements" that life is maintained expressing our submission to God and in Him.

So then, what defines the word atmosphere best?

1. An envelope of gases surrounding the earth or another planet.
2. A surrounding or pervading mood, environment, or influence.

The word 'atmosphere' is derived from the Greek root "atmos," which comes from the root "awet-mo" meaning to "to blow, inspire, spiritually arouse."[51]

We can quickly distinguish the three elements that comprise an atmosphere: the envelope, the gases and the influence or pull (gravity). In the context of Heaven's atmosphere, we see that:

The envelope is our spirit
The gases are the elements of our spiritual identity
The pull of gravity is the fear of the Lord

## THE ENVELOPE

The envelope or container of the atmosphere is released by our spirit through our fellowship either with God or that which we are in fellowship with.

When we have Acknowledged God, we have invited the Holy Spirit to enter our present circumstances, and thereby establish an atmosphere of heaven. Everything that is alive exists in an atmosphere.

*"So we fix our eyes not on what is seen, but on what is unseen, since what is seen is temporary, but what is unseen is eternal."* 2 Cor 4:18

---

[51] It is extraordinary how the word atmosphere is originally a spiritually derived word.

Whether it is the air we breathe – either physically or spiritually – or the environment we are in, everything exists within an atmosphere that covers us, sustains us and contains us.

The atmosphere of Acknowledgement is essential because we, as new creations, require the Breath of God to energize our spirit and to sustain the heartbeat of our new identity.

Positionally, through this new identity, we become an invading army and a threat to the works of the enemy. We can't hope to be effective if we can't or don't breathe the oxygen of heaven. Acknowledgement makes every Christian a potential and imminent threat to the works of darkness.

## THE ELEMENTS OF OUR SPIRITUAL IDENTITY

In the first chapter of his letters to the church in Ephesus,[52] Paul articulates several of the elements (or better still molecules) of our spiritual identity:

Blessed vs..3
Chosen vs. 4
Predestined vs. 5
Adopted vs. 5
Accepted vs. 6
Redeemed vs. 7
Known by God vs. 9
Inheritors vs. 11
Sealed vs. 13

## THERE ARE TWO KINDS OF GRAVITY

Atmospheres contain sources of gravity. The definition of gravity: the force of attraction by which terrestrial bodies tend to fall toward the center of a mass that is greater than itself.

---

52 Ephesians chapter 1

There are two spiritual gravities: the gravity of God and the gravity of sin. Both are real and have palpable effects. The fear of the Lord keeps us functioning under the influence of the Holy Spirit; and the fear man which releases the power of sin and unbelief.

"The remarkable thing about God is that when you fear God, you fear nothing else, whereas if you do not fear God, you fear everything else." – Oswald Chambers

The two Scriptures that reference these two "gravitational forces" are found in the New Testament:

*For our light affliction, which is but for a moment, works for us a far more exceeding and eternal weight of glory.* 2 Co 4:17

*Wherefore seeing we also are compassed about with so great a cloud of witnesses, let us lay aside every weight, and the sin which doth so easily beset us, and let us run with patience the race that is set before us.* Hebrews 12:1

## THE FEAR OF THE LORD

The fear of the Lord is foundational to any sustained move of the Lord. It is nearly 20 years since John Bevere's watershed book *The Fear of the Lord* was published. I firmly believe it is one of the seminal pieces of spiritual literature. It shook the worlds that it touched. Bevere writes, regarding the nature of spiritual gravity, the fear of the Lord is what sustains heaven and earth:

"I had always seen the love of God as the foundation for relationship with the Lord. I quickly discovered that the fear of the Lord was just as foundational. Isaiah writes,

> *'The Lord is exalted, for he dwells on high;*
> *he will fill Zion with his justice and righteousness.*
> *He will be the sure foundation for your times,*
> *a rich store of salvation and wisdom and knowledge;*
> *the fear of the Lord is the key to this treasure.'* Isaiah 33:5-6 NIV

Holy fear is the key to God's sure foundation, unlocking the treasuries of salvation, wisdom and knowledge."[53]

Both gravities affect what we see, feel, believe, do and expect. But if the fear of the Lord is a life-giving and life-sustaining 'meal,' the fear of man is like a sugar high, short, non-nutritious and leading to long-term toxicity. Both have gravitational pulls.

In the case of Elijah, the fear of the Lord launched him into a ministry that thwarted the demonic enemies of the God of Israel at a critical time. "Elijah had developed biblical values, priorities and eternal perspectives that had captured his heart which then controlled what he did with his life. As a result, he acted on his faith by following God's call."[54]

The fear of man surrenders to the forces of sight, appetites and power.

The fear of God is a voluntary submission to the authority of God by faith, the promise of grace by the Cross and the power of the Spirit through prayer.

The gravity to which we are most yielded is the one that will manifest and prevail.

## THE FEAR OF MAN

"When we protect our own turf, when we get our eyes on people and what they have done or said, we fail to see God at work." Hampton Keathley III

When we fail to recognize and come under the influence of God, we have veered off course and out of orbit and choose to yield to our own orbits (lust of the flesh, lust of the eyes and the pride of life).

Keathley continues, "We become blind to the work of God. All we see are the conditions. When this happens, we are unable to respond with the right kind of action – with ministry, endurance and faith… Becoming personality-oriented nearly always leads to another consequence… they

---

53 John Bevere, *The Fear of the Lord*, p. xv
54 Hampton J. Keathley III, https://bible.org/seriespage/17-taking-your-mantle-1-kings-1919-21

either brag about the person they admire… or they attack and criticize, bringing persecution and heartache. When God is not the focus, we lose."

We are all impacted by both. This is very similar to the two gravities that we come under in addition to earth's: the gravity of the sun and the gravity of the moon.

Both kinds of gravity impact certain aspects of the earth: the moon affects the tides of the oceans while the sun is responsible for the rotation of the earth, its seasons, its days and nights, and its temperatures. Though the moon does reflect light, that of the sun, it has no light of its own. It is a dead planet.

Hampton Keathley presents this dichotomy of gravities in the passage in the Bible in 1 Kings 19 when the great prophet Elijah called fire down from heaven and slew the 450 prophets of Baal, but he then succumbs to the threats of Jezebel after the great victory.

Keathley says, "Unable to hurt the Lord, Jezebel did what Satan and people always do. She attacked the instrument and gave vent to her hatred and malice. She sent a messenger with her threat… Elijah's action is totally out of character, but it serves to remind us again of everyone's vulnerability – that we must each take heed lest we fall."[55]

Gravity is determined by the point of our focus, which will impact our expectation of God's manifestation. God is generous to those who remain under His gravitational pull. Just look at these benefits that also impact not only our atmosphere but those who are within its influence.

The gravity of the fear of the Lord is the glue that holds everything together. In studying this aspect of atmosphere, it becomes apparent to me that the gravity of the spirit realm is the fear of the Lord. The fear of the Lord is a catalytic force that expresses the attributes of the Almighty God through these expressions.

We can examine the interaction of these 3 aspects of Atmosphere – our spirit, our identity and the fear of God – in the context of Genesis chapter 1.

---

[55] Hampton Keathley III, https://bible.org/seriespage/15-crisis-elijah-1-kings-194-14

## PROBLEM: ATMOSPHERIC TOXICITY

The first appearance of Acknowledgement applied occurs in Genesis 1:2 when the earth is described as "...without form, and void; and darkness was upon the face of the deep." The American Standard Version translates it, "And the earth was waste and void; and darkness was upon the face of the deep." v. 2a

## RESOLUTION: ATMOSPHERIC REPLACEMENT

Every solution involves the introduction of a pattern concomitant with a specific sequence of actions.[56] Take a look at this sequence:

## ACKNOWLEDGEMENT

The Bible accurately Acknowledges and reveals the condition of the earth; it was not capable of sustaining life. We don't know what happened to make it so; the Bible is silent about it. According to the legal dictionary, "To acknowledge is to admit, affirm, declare, testify, avow, confess, or own as genuine..."[57] By stating what it is, the condition was then subjected to change. Before an alcoholic can ever hope to have victory, he must Acknowledge his condition. According to Alcoholics Anonymous, this principle of Acknowledgement is the core foundation to sobriety, since whenever a person speaks in an AA meeting; they all do so with this salutation: Hi, my name is Joe (or Mary) and I am an alcoholic. The principle being: you can only overcome what you are willing to Acknowledge.

In Genesis 1, God illustrates to us how Acknowledgement starts with the admission of the condition, which is quickly followed by a corresponding redemptive action for that condition; the necessity for a new atmosphere:

*"And the Spirit of God moved upon the face of the waters."* Gen 1:2.

---

[56] Hebrews 8:5 "He says, 'See that you make all things according to the pattern which was shown you on the mountain.'"

[57] Free Legal Dictionary - http://legal-dictionary.thefreedictionary.com/acknowledgment

## DECLARATION

God's response to the problem of "waste, and void and darkness" is to introduce an atmospheric shift that contains and sustains the solution. **The Holy Spirit is the forerunner of transformation.**

This second action, following God's Acknowledgement of the circumstances, begins with the introduction of His Holy Spirit into the situation. This is immediately followed by His proclamation, *"Let there be light."* Genesis1:3

The Spirit contains all 3 elements for a sustainable atmosphere:

* An envelope (we are sealed by the Holy Spirit, Eph. 1:13),
* The sustaining air (man does not live by bread alone, Deu. 8:3),
* The pull/gravity (able to withstand in the evil day, and having done all, to stand. Stand therefore, Eph. 6:13-4).

Each and every divine shift (revival) begins with the atmospheric change that is initiated when God breathes and speaks into the situation, making Acknowledgement Divine CPR [Cardiopulmonary resuscitation].[58]

## THE BREATH OF GOD

The Hebrew word for spirit and breath is the same word: 'ruwach.' The spiritual metaphor of breath for God's Holy Spirit is one that is carried throughout Scripture.[59]

There are at least 4 instances in which the 'ruwach' of God is released with the same transformational effect – the first being right here in Genesis 1:2, *"And the Spirit [ruwach] of God was hovering over the face of the waters."*[60]

---

[58] CPR is a lifesaving technique useful in many emergencies, including heart attack or near drowning, in which someone's breathing or heartbeat has stopped.

[59] Jesus is described as The Door, but I believe that it is the Spirit that comes through the windows of our lives that gives us great light and life.

[60] **Second:** Gen 2:7 And the LORD God formed man of the dust of the ground, and breathed into his nostrils the breath of life; and man became a living soul; **Third:** Ez 37:5 Thus saith the Lord GOD unto these bones; Behold, I will cause breath to enter into you, and ye shall

The intention of God's response was to initiate a redemptive outcome – a creation He called "good."

When we are instructed to Acknowledge God in Proverbs 3:6, we are following the pattern of what God did when the earth was *"waste and void; and darkness was upon the face of the deep."* So with our breath (our words) and a declaration of God's dominion over the situation, we introduce the breath of God, releasing heaven's atmosphere.

## OUR CONFESSIONS: WORDS THAT LEAD US OUT WILL BE THE WORDS THAT LEAD US IN

Part of the definition of Acknowledgement is spiritual declaration. Declaration is what occurs when we declare and confess that something (a territory, district, situation, etc.) is subject to a particular legal jurisdiction – heaven.

*"I acknowledged my sin unto thee, and mine iniquity have I not hid. I said, I will confess my transgressions unto the LORD; and thou forgave the iniquity of my sin."* Psalm 32:5

*"Whosoever therefore shall confess me before men, him will I confess also before my Father which is in heaven."* Matthew 10:32

*"Also I say unto you, Whosoever shall confess me before men, him shall the Son of man also confess before the angels of God.* Luke 12:8

## ACKNOWLEDGEMENT CREATES A THRESHOLD TO HEAVEN

Acknowledgement marks a starting place through the recognition of where we are, BEFORE we can proceed to where we are called. That is exactly where the Bible begins.

This is a practical template for us to apply: Acknowledge and confess where we are and then declare where we are called to be. Even if we don't know what the specific cause of the problem is – by Acknowledging God, we introduce Him into the situation.

---

live; **Fourth:** John 20:22 And when he had said this, he breathed on them, and saith unto them, Receive ye the Holy Ghost.

## CLASHING ATMOSPHERES
Hostile Jamming: The Resistance to an Atmosphere of Acknowledgement:

*"I find then a law, that, when I would do good, evil is present with me."* Romans 7:21

Once the Acknowledgement process is initiated, it attracts the attention of two realms: Heaven and Hell.

We can anticipate hostile jamming because, through the authority of heaven, we represent an imminent threat to Satan's control of his kingdom. We have an enemy who is eager to keep us under the canopy of his atmosphere of deception, which leads to destruction and death.

We see this clash of kingdoms dramatically revealed in Daniel chapter 10. Daniel has been fasting and praying for 3 weeks (21 days) for God to intercede for His people taken captive in Babylon. An angel of the Lord appears to Daniel, saying:

*"Do not fear, Daniel, for from the first day that you set your heart to understand, and to humble yourself before your God, your words were heard; and I have come because of your words.[13] But the* **prince of the kingdom of Persia withstood me twenty-one days**; *and behold, Michael, one of the chief princes, came to help me, for I had been left alone there with the kings of Persia.[14] Now I have come to make you understand what will happen to your people in the latter days, for the vision refers to many days yet to come."* Daniel 10:12-14 NKJV

Here is a picture, boldly portrayed, of two powerful forces of the heavenlies vying for the control of God's people. Daniel's words were heard as soon as they were uttered and the answer to his request was immediately dispatched. However, the means of delivering the **message was intercepted** and a struggle, in the spirit realm, had to be decided before the answer reached Daniel.

*Heaven's answers require heaven's atmospheres.*

There are things that we can and must do and some that only God can do to make sure we do not just survive, but thrive in this battle with the adversary.

## THE ACKNOWLEDGED LIFE

One thing we must do is to daily, intentionally put on proper military gear as detailed in Ephesians 6:11-18.[61]

Once we have our military equipment, we also need to put on our right attitude. Paul instructs us that there is a consistent and ongoing renewal process in which we, as new creations, must engage that he identifies in Romans 12:1-2: *"Be ye not conformed to this world, but be ye transformed by the renewing of your mind, that ye may prove what is that good, and acceptable, and perfect, will of God."*

Just as the mind is not static but capable of being renewed, stretched and changed, scientists have discovered, over the last decade especially, that the human brain is a living organ that grows as it is stimulated.

"The brain is the thought muscle, that is designed to be capable of *learning*; learns through intellect, experiences and impartation. It still amazes me but it's true: Whatever we repeatedly sense and feel and want and think is slowly but surely sculpting neural structure... Much mental and therefore neural activity flows through the brain like ripples on a river, with no lasting effects on its channel. But intense, prolonged, or repeated mental/neural activity – especially if it is conscious – will leave an enduring imprint in real structure, like a surging current reshaping a riverbed... If you stand back from the details of these studies, one simple truth stands out: Your experiences matter."[62]

---

61 *Put on the whole armor of God, that ye may be able to stand against the wiles of the devil. For we wrestle not against flesh and blood, but against principalities, against powers, against the rulers of the darkness of this world, against spiritual wickedness in high places. Wherefore take unto you the whole armor of God, that ye may be able to withstand in the evil day, and having done all, to stand. Stand therefore, having your loins girt about with truth, and having on the breastplate of righteousness; And your feet shod with the preparation of the gospel of peace; Above all, taking the shield of faith, wherewith ye shall be able to quench all the fiery darts of the wicked. And take the helmet of salvation, and the sword of the Spirit, which is the word of God: 18 Praying always with all prayer and supplication in the Spirit, and watching thereunto with all perseverance and supplication for all saints.*

62 Rick Hanson, *Hardwiring Happiness*, p. 10-11

God's design for the Acknowledged Life is meant to be experiential; we go from faith to faith,[63] strength to strength[64] and glory to glory.[65] And when we encounter glory, it is not just an opportunity to build a tabernacle but a means of transformation that involves getting **into** the river, becoming **part of** the river and releasing the river. As Jesus said, *"Out of their bellies will flow rivers of living water."* (John 7:38)

*"There is a river, the streams whereof shall make glad the city of God, the holy place of the tabernacles of the most High."* Psalm 46:4

God designed our brain to be "…like ripples on a river…" When our brain and our spirit flow with the currents of heaven's flow, heaven's power is released over us and our circumstances. **Acknowledgement can serve to reshape the riverbeds of our life**.

As we focus upon these Acknowledgements, particularly the ones the Lord has spoken over us, these declarations become our conversations through prayer. This is how our identities of who we are in Christ are established. *"For in him we live, and move, and have our being."* Acts 17:28

Daily, we must remember that in Acknowledging the attributes of the New Creation, we are admitting, affirming, declaring, testifying, avowing and confessing what God has spoken over us to be true.

## ACTIVATING THE ATMOSPHERE

God has given us Acknowledgements to activate the atmosphere of heaven. They are found throughout the New Testament and specifically in the book of Romans. Paul exhorts us to invoke the following:

We are more than conquerors. (Rom 8:37)
We are redeemed. (Eph 1:7)

---

[63] *"For in it the righteousness of God is revealed from faith to faith; as it is written, 'The just shall live by faith.'"* Rom 1:17
[64] *"They go from strength to strength, Every one of them appears before God in Zion."* Psalm 84:7
[65] *"But we all, with unveiled face, beholding as in a mirror the glory of the Lord, are being transformed into the same image from glory to glory, just as from the Lord, the Spirit."* 2 Cor 3:18

## THE ACKNOWLEDGED LIFE

We are a new creation. (2 Cor 5:17)
In Christ, we are blessed. (Eph 1:3)
We are predestined. (Eph 1:5)
We are called. (Rom 1:6 et al.)
We are justified. (Rom 3:24)
We are glorified. (Rom 8:30)
We are unable to be separated from God. (Rom 8:35)

### THE CREATIVE FORCE OF OUR WORDS

What we proclaim and declare over ourselves and our circumstances may not appear to exist in the moment but again, it represents the threshold through which we enter into the realm of believing God is at work.

These statements also place us into agreement with God. Agreement is a powerful corollary principle of Acknowledgement. What we achieve isn't accomplished at the point we make the declaration, but releases a confession of faith into the future.

E.W. Kenyon made some excellent points about the value of such Acknowledgements:

> "We are to confess what we are in Christ.
> To confess that you are redeemed.
> Confessing your righteousness.
> Few of us realize the effect of our spoken word on our own heart or on our Adversary.
> No one ever rises above it.
> You become dangerous to the Adversary when you become strong enough to resist him – when you have learned to trust in the ability of the Father to meet your every need.
> Our faith never goes beyond our confession."[66]

---

66 E.W. Kenyon, *In His Presence*

Confessions and declarations also take the form of worship, which is an expression of Acknowledgement that is sung (or danced or painted or acted) instead of spoken. So significant is worship in sustaining the atmosphere of heaven, it is the environment for:

Healing
Deliverance
Prophesy
Miracles
Visions

The Book of Psalms comprises the largest book of the Bible. Let us remember that the Psalms are worship songs. So powerful was the atmosphere of worship in his life that it actually catapulted David into his destiny – warrior/king.

Royalty is then a produced-quality that David demonstrated; before any crown touched his head, worship streamed from his heart. David was anointed as Israel's king when he was a boy, probably in his early teens, but he would have to wait until he turned 30 before becoming king of Judah. Royalty is manifested over a consistent period of time.

"David's preparation for kingship was found in serving a demonized king who sought to kill him. His servant leadership was further cultivated in the desert, where he found himself leading an army of discontented men who were distressed and in debt. Through adverse circumstances and the challenges of personal weakness, in rejection and favor, the Lord cultivated a leader through whom He could truly rule."[67] Mike Bickle

## THE 4 ATMOSPHERIC DISTURBANCES

1. Atmosphere of Discouragement
2. Atmosphere of Impatience

---

[67] http://mikebickle.org/resources/series/leadership-lessons-from-the-life-of-david

3. Atmosphere of Denial and Complacency
4. Atmosphere of Temporary Success

## 1. ATMOSPHERE OF DISCOURAGEMENT
*Discouragement is a Spiritual Atmosphere*

God knew that we would encounter periods of disappointment and delay. Often discouragement enters when our own alarm clock called 'expectation' rings, and the period of testing still continues. That is why we are instructed by the word to Acknowledge Him in all of our ways. Once we become born-again, we are no longer privates in an army, but royalty in His Majesty's Service.

Acknowledgement isn't something we do only at the beginning or at the end; Acknowledging is something that we must continue to do throughout God's process, especially in the middle.

"Everything looks like a failure in the middle. Everyone loves inspiring beginnings and happy endings; it is just the middles that involve hard work."[68]

**Acknowledgement is hard work**. Acknowledgement functions as heaven's spiritual fitness program, but it is also a precursor to us being prepared to function in a hostile territory which carries with it a hostile atmosphere.

Here are some facts to remember when an atmosphere of discouragement decides to come by for an unannounced visit:

* Discouragement is a temporary atmosphere; it is subject to change.
* We don't have to adopt it. We may have to ignore its leaning on the buzzer of our emotions. In all instances, we must refuse to answer its call!
* Remember: we know Jesus, and more importantly, Jesus knows us!
* We have a covenant with Jesus, signed in the Blood of Christ!
* We have a promise that no weapon formed against us shall prosper!

---
[68] Rosabeth Moss Canter

Enforce it!

* Don't get into a conversation with discouragement (as Eve did).
* Get and keep the helmet of salvation (your mindset) on!

Have in place a regular time of worship, to recharge your atmosphere. Worship is like a spiritual air purifier. The Psalms are great for this:

*"Bless the LORD, O my soul,*
*and forget not all His benefits:*
*Who forgives all your iniquities,*
*Who heals all your diseases,*
*Who redeems your life from destruction,*
*Who crowns you with lovingkindness and tender mercies,*
*Who satisfies your mouth with good things,*
*So that your youth is renewed like the eagle's."* (Psalm 103:2-5)
*"For in him we live, and move, and have our being"* Acts 17:28

## 2. THE SPIRITUAL ATMOSPHERE OF IMPATIENCE | STUBBORNNESS | IMMOBILITY

Impatience: defined as not willing to wait for something or someone.[69] Impatience is an unspoken indictment of God for failure to abide by His agreements. Eve clearly was a victim of the spiritual atmosphere of impatience.

"God is not neutral or care-less about the importance of patience. In fact, Scripture often uses patience as an indicator of where a person will spend eternity, in heaven or in hell. Patience! It would seem that our patience, or our impatience, is much more than just a personality trait. Our level of patience says everything about us,"[70] states Ryan Haider.

---

69 http://www.merriam-webster.com/dictionary/impatient
70 Ryan Haider, http://bit.ly/2et3pTN

The New Testament exhorts us to walk in the Spirit in a manner referred to as patience. Patience is a quality of wise controlled restraint. "Biblical patience is a Spirit-enabled calmness that one possesses and exhibits in the midst of an unpleasant circumstance because they are convinced of God's sovereign, good, and meticulous care."[71]

Patience is definitely a virtue; and stubborn impatience clearly a gateway to hell.

## STUBBORNNESS

On the other hand, stubbornness is a rejection of God's sovereignty that defies God's leadership. Just because you are somewhere in God doesn't mean that it is a permanent residence. One of the lessons to be had in the wilderness desert is: the wilderness was not a destination; it was an assignment that involved learning specific lessons that would prove to be valuable in the future.

Spiritual mobility is another expression of Acknowledging God. Acknowledgement is a way of expressing that we are ready, willing and able to wait upon God. But in this digital culture, we have been conditioned to have it our way, right away: fast food and fast faith. The New Testament does not teach us that we can have it our way! Once things start to go our way, we have little interest in changing it. Christianity, someone once said, is about waiting; and then moving when God moves.

"The sin of impatience reveals our desire to be in control by desiring others to conform to our expectations. If that is true, then the events in our lives are not necessarily the things that cause impatience, they are just the means by which the sin of control is manifested in our lives."[72]

To see God in a wilderness, you must be willing to search for the lesson. What were the lessons for the Hebrews?

First, manna – God wanted them to be totally reliant upon Him in the upcoming Promised Land rather than the land and its fertility.

---

71  Ryan Haider, http://bit.ly/2et3pTN
72  Casey Lewis https://christianitymatters.com/2012/09/27/respectable-sins-impatience-irritability/

Second, they needed to make God the center, not the periphery of their lives.

Third, they must maintain their separation with the inhabitants of the land (don't intermarry) since God didn't want them adopting any pagan rites or gods.

## IMMOBILITY

A fourth lesson the Lord wanted them to learn well is to be able to follow the Lord's presence. The Lord didn't give them a map with an AAA card. They needed to learn to follow the presence, not stay immobile in one place.

Spiritual interruptions are one of the ways that God makes His Presence and Goodness known.

**Once a particular spiritual cycle is completed, expect a new one.** Be sensitive to the intransigent spiritual atmosphere of the "that's how we do things around here" syndrome. I call this form of immobility 'old wine syndrome'; we get too comfortable with traditions and with the victories of the past.

Once we develop a spiritual rhythm, there is a flow that begins to emerge, and out of the flow come habits, routines, and a sense of well-being. However, the danger is we can let stagnation set in.

Habits are good to the degree they engender an intimacy with God, His word and His Spirit. They can even flow from a victory we have in our walk. Yet, when we become too comfortable with the traditions that flowed from the victories of the past, we lose our spiritual agility.

When our habits, rhythms, routines and traditions become the things upon which we rely instead of our daily dialogue with the Lord, we make ourselves vulnerable, especially when you consider the enemy is also described as an Angel of light.

We need to reject the idea that obedience is doing the same thing, day in and day out; no, obedience is doing the right thing, day in and day out.

*"I sought the LORD, and He answered me, And delivered me from all my fears. They looked to Him and were radiant, And their faces will never be ashamed...."* Psalm 34:4-5

We must be vigilant to emulate everything Paul says to do in 2 Timothy 4:2:

*"Preach the word; be ready in season and out of season; reprove, rebuke, exhort, with great patience and instruction."*

Jesus in John 4 demonstrates a high level of spiritual mobility.

He left Judea and went away again into Galilee.

## AND HE HAD TO PASS THROUGH SAMARIA.

*"So He came to a city of Samaria called Sychar, near the parcel of ground that Jacob gave to his son Joseph; and Jacob's well was there. So Jesus, being wearied from His journey, was sitting thus by the well. It was about the sixth hour. There came a woman of Samaria to draw water. Jesus said to her, "Give Me a drink."* John 4:3-7

Jesus was going to Galilee to preach to the Jews, not to a Samaritan woman; and yet in this passage Jesus shows us that following God sometimes involves detours that change history.

*Jesus said to them, "My food is to do the will of Him who sent Me and to accomplish His work".* John 4:34

Judging from Scripture, we have to remain agile enough to be mobile.

Jacob remained agile in order to send his whole family into Egypt.

Joseph and Mary were spiritually agile enough so that Joseph didn't divorce Mary when she was pregnant with Jesus, and when he was instructed to leave Bethlehem and go to Egypt to protect the child Jesus. Though it appeared that this was putting God in reverse, he Acknowledged the instruction given, and returned back to Israel when instructed to do so.

## MY OWN STORY OF CHANGE IN THE WILDERNESS

In my own life, I have had some directional changes. Back in 1979, I was an aspiring playwright. The biggest entertainment company in the world was Warner Communications. It was huge.

Well, after I became a follower of Christ, I was able to get a job there as a temp employee; and God miraculously provided the occasion for me to get a job as a play scout for Warner Theatre Productions. I got to be part of several significant productions: an Arthur Miller play and the production of *Crimes of the Heart*, written by Beth Henley, which went on to win the Pulitzer Prize. At Warner we also discovered John Patrick Shanley, who went on to write the Oscar-winning film *Moonstruck*.

But after 2 years of 60+ hours a week, it was getting old. I kept praying and asking the Lord, "Help me!" And during my prayer He actually answered me when I told him I wanted to leave. He said, "Leave!"

"Leave? I can't just leave. I don't know where to go or what to do. My boss loves me. I can't. You are going to have to help me."

The answer came back quickly, "OK." That was it.

I walked into work the next day, and my boss, the Tony-Award-winner producer, walked in and said, "Anthony, I want to see you in my office."

The first thing she said to me was, "It's not working. I am letting you go."

I said as if I was in a dream (and thinking, Boy, You didn't waste any time, did You?), "OK."

She was shocked. "What are you going to do?"

"I don't know, either advertising or Wall Street."

"Who do you know who is going to get you a job?"

"No one."

She stared back at me as if I were some sort of alien being. I left her office, and within a few months was working on the New York Stock Exchange.

Following God will always stretch you in more ways than one.

## 3. THE HOSTILE ATMOSPHERES OF DENIAL AND COMPLACENCY
## THE ATMOSPHERE OF DENIAL

This atmosphere can begin with our lack of mobility as covered in number two, but then will deteriorate into denial and complacency.

Denial is characterized as a defense mechanism by which a person unconsciously negates the existence of a disease or other stress-producing reality in his or her environment by disavowing thoughts, feelings, etc.

THE ACKNOWLEDGED LIFE

Spiritual denial creates a vacuum whereby a vital lesson from God is not being learned. When we fail to learn a lesson, we are led into the wilderness for a spiritual tutorial… kind of like an academy of the Holy Spirit.

## THE WILDERNESS

When we ignore the things that are happening to us, we do so at our own peril. Denial is seeing the signs and ignoring what the signs are intending to communicate.

That is why the Hebrews spent 40 years in the desert; it was the spiritual atmosphere of denial that deprived them of their destiny.

***An unacknowledged life will always result in slavery.***

The Hebrews were slaves who didn't know they were enslaved! They thought they were victims of history instead of children of God. They were slaves even before they got to Egypt; they were slaves of themselves, their lusts, their actions, motives and so on.

God allowed them to stay in Egypt for over 400 years. The Lord was trying to teach them that it wasn't the Egyptians' fault they were slaves. When they came into Egypt, they all got some choice real estate and opportunity to thrive. But something happened over the centuries. They lost their land, their jobs, and all the benefits that Joseph had gotten for them.

Even with all their spiritual history with God through Abraham, Isaac and Jacob, they couldn't see that it was their thinking and their hearts that made them slaves. It wasn't until Jesus came in the flesh that God got His second point across: you not only need My help, but you need My love (and oh, by the way, I want yours as well).

For 40 years the Israelites were filled with a never-ending cycle of fits and starts with a purpose of embedding into them a culture of Acknowledgement.

Even in the way He configured their order around the Tabernacle of the Presence, God was trying to make a visual statement about the way they needed to be living, with God in the center. If He is not our focus, we will end up being lost instead of being led.

## SPIRITUAL WARFARE AND COMPLACENCY

An example of spiritual denial is failure to Acknowledge and recognize that we live within a spiritual combat zone.

There are many believers who choose to divert or deny the existence of a spiritual adversary because it will necessitate an action and plan to contest the adversity.

*"Be of sober spirit, be on the alert. Your adversary, the devil, prowls around like a roaring lion, seeking someone to devour. But resist him, firm in your faith, knowing that the same experiences of suffering are being accomplished by your brethren who are in the world. After you have suffered for a little while, the God of all grace, who called you to His eternal glory in Christ, will Himself perfect, confirm, strengthen and establish you."* 1 Peter 5:8-10

St. Paul probably was buffeted by Satan as much or more than any other Apostle, so much so that he went to the Lord 3 times about it, to which Jesus tells him that His grace is sufficient for him.

Denial is more common than we want to believe. I think that denial is like morning breath: we all have it, and to solve it requires a simple solution - brush our teeth to remove the film and residue in our mouths and 'renew' our breath. Same thing with denial; we need to wash our minds with the washing of the word of God, and get filled up with His Spirit.

How do we know that we are in spiritual denial?

## SIGNS OF DENIAL

We think that we are in control of our lives.
We have stopped asking God for help.
We no longer have a spiritual hunger for the Scriptures.
We try to control things we can't and ignore things we need to change.
We dismiss what we don't want to see.
We've got all the answers we need. We like to give lots of advice.
We are secretive about what we can't control.
We are habitually stressed out.

We have a habit of being short with people.

I would also offer these 3 Scriptures to put into practice:

> *Prov 4:23 Watch over your heart with all diligence, For from it flow the springs of life.*
> *Col 4:2 Devote yourselves to prayer, keeping alert in it with an attitude of thanksgiving.*
> *Deut 4:9 Only give heed to yourself and keep your soul diligently.*

We must keep in mind that the Lord's mercies are new every morning for a very good reason – so are the attacks.

## HUMILITY | ACKNOWLEDGEMENT | CONFESSION

Acknowledgement allows us to see ourselves with greater objectivity.

It is an expression of personal humility. This blog post says it best:

"Humility is a virtue [because] it takes a tremendous amount of humility to question your assumptions and admit that you were wrong. It's really uncomfortable, so most people just avoid it."[73] Nick Bartlett

A good sign that humility is in operation is when we learn to overcome and recognize stubbornness, negative bias and pride in ourselves. Acknowledgement keeps our heads spiritually clear and mentally aligned to hear God, fear God and stay near God.

## THE ATMOSPHERE OF COMPLACENCY

Complacency is described as a self-satisfied state of negligence or carelessness, especially in relation to one's personal situation.

People who experience small incremental changes over a sufficient period of time tend to become complacent and unaware that their situation has changed. Because the changes are so gradual and small, they may

---
[73] Nick Bartlett labs.openviewpartners.com/are-you-open-to-being-wrong/

not even recognize the consequences, and the modified situation simply becomes perceived as the "new normal."

The spiritual counterfeit of Godly contentment is complacency. This is the sin of the churches of Ephesus and Laodicea as referenced in the book of Revelation.

The Church of Ephesus lost its first love, and the Church of Laodicea is accused of being lukewarm: both of which were spiritually unacceptable to the Lord.

According to Jim Renke, "Complacency is rooted in an attitude of self-sufficiency. We tend to think we can handle life and what it brings us. We trust in our own ability to understand, decide and act. We believe that constant dependence on God is either a dream or a nightmare, but not a reality we should experience."[74]

He also sees complacency as an acceptance and comfort within a culture of compromise. Another view of complacency is when we begin to derive spiritual satisfaction without real spiritual victory.

## 4. THE ATMOSPHERE OF TEMPORARY SUCCESS
### Our Successes, Our Titles, Our Bank Accounts

I believe when we enjoy any degree of success spiritually, that doesn't automatically entitle us to any spiritual perks or benefits. But it is true that when we experience it, it can feel like "we have arrived."

Success is simply a plateau that occurs after successfully scaling a mountain that has resisted our faith for a period of time.

Why is it that our successes separate us from the Lord? One reason is that **success is often not a reward, but a test.** Can we be trusted with the authority that is attached to success? Can we be trusted with finances? Can we be trusted with the marriage?

---

[74] Jim Renke https://jimrenke.com/2013/02/13/4-signs-of-spiritual-complacency/

## THE ACKNOWLEDGED LIFE

Here is a simple success audit: as a result of the success, are you closer to God or are you closer to your success? I believe our Father has many blessings that He is just waiting to give to us.

Here is an example of that kind of Father Love. It concerns a father who was fishing on the lake near my house in New Jersey.

I was out mowing my lawn when I saw my neighbor's son fishing in our lake. His name is Bob. That morning, he no sooner dropped his line into the lily pad part of the lake than he felt a hit on his line. Sure enough, he had one.

But Bob, being the kind of father that he is (a good one), didn't reel it in.

No, he placed the rod in the holder and casually walked back home and saw his daughter.

He told her he had to come back to get something, but would she be nice enough to go check on his fishing rod for him.

No sooner did she head out to the planted fishing rod, and then she picked it up, and to her delight, realized that there was a fish on the other end.

She called back to the house, saying, "Daddy. Daddy. I got one."

Bob smiled.

She walked back to the house with a smile as broad as a six-lane Jersey highway, saying, "Look, Dad. I got one."

Bob grinned as well and said, "You sure did."

She said, "This is the biggest fish I ever caught."

"No doubt. No doubt."

The big catch completely turned the day around for her and Bob: they weren't just visiting Grandma, they were on an adventure. But it just so happened that the adventure was just across the street.

That one fish changed the atmosphere of that day for Bob, his daughter and Grandma.

When we Acknowledge God, we remind ourselves that before we arrived at today, God was already there. And He already had a fishing pole, complete with the fish on the line, already prepared for us.

I believe that if we would just Acknowledge Him, we might hear Him say more often, "Go check on this customer for Me." Or "Go down to the school for Me." "Call up your mother for Me." Only to discover the outcome is an unexpected delight.

Can you believe the Lord has 'fishing poles planted' all over for His kids? He's just waiting for us to Acknowledge Him. "Where did you put the fishing pole today, Dad?"

## THE DANGERS OF THE ATMOSPHERE OF SUCCESS

Oftentimes, success comes through our understanding and knowledge. Peter had some firsthand knowledge of this when he was the first disciple to proclaim that Jesus was not only the Messiah, but the Son of God.

What happened after this is pretty interesting: Jesus says, in front of everyone, that He is changing Peter's name from Simon, which means "reed," to Peter, which means "rock," and that Jesus was commencing a building program on this.

When Jesus tells everyone that He is going to be crucified, Peter defies this revelation, which causes Peter immediately to get sent to the back of the line. "But he turned, and said unto Peter, Get thee behind me, Satan: thou art an offence unto me: for thou savors not the things that be of God." Matthew 16:23

None of us have 'arrived' – there are always new roads God is looking to have us travel, no matter what victories we have championed for the Gospel.

## IN RECAP OF THIS CHAPTER ON ATMOSPHERES

Everything exists within an atmosphere.

Acknowledgement releases the atmosphere of heaven into our own atmosphere.

When we Acknowledge God, it creates a threshold to the kingdom of God.

We will experience adversarial atmospheres.
Our words are our weapons.
We will encounter at least 4 different kinds of atmospheric disturbances: Discouragement, Impatience, Denial and Complacency.

## THE 4 PURPOSES OF A SPIRITUAL WILDERNESS:

To bring awareness to an unseen condition
To reposition God back into the center of your life
To expose to you where you are
To remind you of your destination

## PRAYER OF ACKNOWLEDGEMENT

Lord, I thank You for where I am. As long as I can reach up to the hope of heaven, I am rich, wealthy and gloriously blessed! Please continue to walk me through every situation with a deeper understanding that nothing can or will separate me from You, Your purpose and Your promises. Your Acknowledgement of me made the way for my Acknowledgement of You. Thank you, God, for the Gift of Acknowledgement.

*Jesus said, And if I go and prepare a place for you, I will come again, and receive you unto myself; that where I am, there ye may be also.* John 14:3

*What shall we then say to these things? If God be for us, who can be against us? He that spared not his own Son, but delivered him up for us all, how shall he not with him also freely give us all things? Who shall lay anything to the charge of God's elect? It is God that justifies... Who shall separate us from the love of Christ? Shall tribulation, or distress, or persecution, or famine, or nakedness, or peril, or sword? As it is written, For thy sake we are killed all the day long; we are accounted as sheep for the slaughter. Nay, in all these things we are more than conquerors through him that loved us. For I am persuaded, that neither death, nor life, nor angels, nor principalities, nor powers, nor things present, nor things to come, Nor height, nor depth, nor any other creature, shall be able to separate us from the love of God, which is in Christ Jesus our Lord.* Romans 8:31-33, 35-39

## *Chapter 14*

# THE ARK OF CHARACTER

## ACKNOWLEDGEMENT

Today, I Acknowledge that my thoughts, actions and motives reflect an eternal purpose. Character is my response to God in the present. The goal of my Acknowledgement is to become a master, disciple and leader of each moment.

## KEY POINTS

* By Acknowledging God, I move forward
* The Acknowledged mind is a renewed mind, one that can demonstrate the exploits of heaven
* The Acknowledged Life makes a difference, not only for me, but for those with me and after me
* The Acknowledged Life repurposes my past defeats into testimonies of character that keep me resilient

I believe character is the evidence of an Acknowledged Life. Character is more than doing the right thing – that's a machine. Character is something alive, organic, and as a function gives life to the things within its environment. Like Jesus: wherever He went, He had a habit of giving life to those who came into contact with Him.

Everyone possesses some level of character. We are all at different stages. We all presume that because we have a body, it just comes with a character. Like a complete set. Wrong. Character doesn't come fully assembled.

And just because we know about it doesn't mean we possess it.

The thing about character: it's not a function of education. Otherwise we would be able to educate ourselves into righteousness. Rather character only comes through the process of living an obedient life. Obedience is an expression of intent, action and motive carried out under the direction of God. *"Though He were a son He learned obedience through the things which He suffered."* Hebrews 5:8

We are not the first folks to be tricked into thinking that all we need is information to create a moral life. Way back in the Garden, Eve saw this knowledge tree and figured it was a shortcut to glory.

*"But of the tree of the knowledge of good and evil, thou shalt not eat of it: for in the day that thou eat thereof thou shalt surely die."* Genesis 2:17

*"...the woman saw that the tree was good for food, and that it was pleasant to the eyes, and a tree to be desired to make one wise, she took of the fruit thereof, and did eat, and gave also unto her husband with her; and he did eat."* Genesis 3:6

Well, we all know how that turned out. Forced from the Garden after foreclosure proceedings, the first family discovered the consequences of disobedience. And the temptation continues to today.

*"But I see another law at work in my body, warring against the law of my mind and holding me captive to the law of sin that dwells within me. 24 What a wretched man I am! Who will rescue me from this body of death? 25 Thanks be to God, through Jesus Christ our Lord! So then, with my mind I serve the law of God, but with my flesh I serve the law of sin."* Romans 7:23

## THE MYTH ABOUT CHARACTER

Everyone believes they have a handle on their character, until they realize it is too late. Character, like experience, is something you discover right after you need it. Somehow or another, we have also been led to believe that character is a knowledge-asset, instead of a social-spiritual asset.

By extricating God from our culture (and our accountability to Him), the idea has taken hold that character is obsolete and replaced with ability. Our philosophy of self-determination undercuts the spiritual nature of character. Now our society is obsessed with striving to create our own status as digital celebrities through our own efforts.

And so today, our revered Ivy League schools are lauded for their intellectual pursuits instead of their original spiritual mandate to disseminate the Gospel.[75] The secular shift across all these institutions has degraded their mission from the quest for transformation to simply the pursuit of information.

## CHARACTER BEGINS WITH KNOWING THE CREATOR

*"We speak wisdom, however, among them that are full grown: yet a wisdom not of this world, nor of the rulers of this world, who are coming to naught: but we speak God's wisdom in a mystery, [even] the [wisdom] that hath been hidden, which God foreordained before the worlds unto our glory: which none of the rulers of this world hath known: for had they known it, they would not have crucified the Lord of glory: but as it is written,* **Things which eye saw not, and ear heard not, And [which] entered not into the heart of man, Whatsoever things God prepared for them that love him.** *But unto us God revealed [them] through the Spirit: for the Spirit searches all things, yea, the deep things of God… For who hath known the mind of the Lord, that he should instruct him? But we have the mind of Christ."* 1 Cor 2:6-10, 16

As stated earlier, obedience is expression of intent, action and motive carried out under the direction of God. That expression is only possible through a relationship with God and is referred to in the New Testament as koninia. It is the Greek word that means communion, joint participation with other believers and participation with the Spirit of God.

---

75 Seven of the eight Ivy League schools were founded as seminaries.

Koinina is fellowship; but since God is a Father, His long-term objective is a great big family reunion.

Koininia is the atmosphere God provides for the purpose of not only encountering Him but empowering us to function as sons and daughters of God. That is why our spiritual, intimate daily encounters with Him are so vital.

In the same way, commission of sin becomes a generational curse, entering into koininia becomes a generational blessing, manifesting into character.

Consequently, the character of God's kingdom is then reflected by the combination of traits and qualities that distinguish Who God is and the new nature of the new creation.

As we grow in our relationship with Christ through our union with Him, change or rather spiritual renovation begins taking place.

I believe that the obsession with home renovation today reflects the very thing that God is doing with His family: the Church. And instead of flipping houses, God's flipping characters.

The 'art' behind the way that these gifted artisans and craftsmen and women are able to take crumbling out-of-date homes and transform them into visions of glory reminds me a great deal of what God does when he gets a hold of our lives: instead of being a home-flipper, he becomes a soul-flipper.

## GOD, THE ORIGINAL HOUSE FLIPPER

*"And the earth was without form, and void; and darkness was upon the face of the deep. And the Spirit of God moved upon the face of the waters."* Genesis 1:2

*"We heard him say, I will destroy this temple that is made with hands, and within three days **I will build another made without hands**."* Mark 14:58 [emphasis mine]

I see God as the original house-flipper. What He did through Jesus, putting our sins on Him and crucifying Him on the cross, was purchasing back our property that was appropriately condemned for the purpose of building us into a completely new structure. *"Therefore if a man be in Christ*

*He is a new creation..."* 2 Cor 5:17 What God starts, God finishes. *"He who has begun a good work in you will complete it until the day of Christ Jesus."* Phil 1:6 NKJV

And character is the restoration of the original intent of the Architect.

After Jesus rose from the dead, He ascended and He began overseeing the most prodigious building project in history - the Church. He then commissioned the Holy Spirit to break ground, with the creation of a new heart.

Character is what God looks to build into every man and woman. Character is the mental, behavioral and spiritual quality distinctive to an individual which releases life, His life, through spiritual relevance and revival.

I suggest that Godly character begins with the Acknowledgement of God, and from that point forward, the Lord begins co-laboring with us into a building project.[76] It's not just about His Church, but is about each individual temple.

Character becomes the end product of the Holy Spirit's spiritual renovation.

*"What? Know ye not that your body is the temple of the Holy Ghost which is in you, which ye have of God, and ye are not your own?"* 1 Cor 6:19

Acknowledgement recognizes we are not our own and redemption is proof of purchase, Christ's purchase.

Redemption then becomes a classic case of a spiritual house flipper who takes a house in foreclosure and converts it into a valuable asset.

## THE CROSS IS HEAVEN'S BUILDER'S SQUARE BY WHICH THE ENTIRE HOUSE IS FRAMED.

*"For whom he did foreknow, he also did* **predestinate to be conformed** *to the image of his Son, that he might be the firstborn among many brethren."* Rom 8:29

---

[76] 1 Corinthians 2:9 For we are God's co-workers in God's service

Everything in the kingdom of God is measured against the same eternal standard: Christ and the cross. The concept that the church is something **we** do is false: Jesus is the church builder.

The cross then becomes God's Builder's Square, but it also aligns us with the purposes of heaven.

## THE ARK: PRECURSOR TO THE CROSS

When Noah was directed to build the ark, it became the structure by which humanity would be preserved. It was made out of wood, as was the cross.

The ark preserved those who entered it; and those who entered the ark were delivered from the flood. However, this required no transformation or change. Those who entered the ark possessed the same character when they left the ark, as they had when they entered it.[77] The ark represented the preserving power of the Abrahamic covenant to maintain his offspring.

Thankfully, God wasn't finished there; He had a greater destination for those who would trust Him to accomplish beyond what man could think, dream or imagine.

Like the Ark, character is the means by which God transports us:

For a Purpose,
Formed in the Present,
Prepared for the Future,
Redeemed and Forsaking the former things,
With the promise of arriving at the desired destination.

Back in Noah's day, there was no other way for someone to survive the coming Flood. The Ark was a new construction, a new design and would take a significant amount of time to construct (120 years). To those who

---

[77] Genesis 19:33 And they made their father drink wine that night: and the firstborn went in, and lay with her father, and he perceived not when she lay down, nor when she arose.

did not understand what was about to take place, it became a useless and functionless apparatus.

When we Acknowledge God it is as if we are entering the Ark of His preservation, His divine process, but instead of going in one way and coming out the same way, we are transformed into the image of His Son.

Acknowledgement is not just a form of submission but it is a spiritual incubator that allows God to produce in us a greater weight of glory.[78]

For me, Acknowledgement is our quest for character [the original design], and that character is Christ. Character is the by-product of the application of the cross in specific areas of our lives. Consider we are born devoid of character in much the same way as in Gen 1:2 *"And the earth was without form, and void; and darkness was upon the face of the deep. And the Spirit of God moved upon the face of the waters."*

Character begins with the Acknowledgement that we are unable to achieve God's standard through our own efforts; in the same way an alcoholic acknowledges he or she is an alcoholic and is unable to control their addiction through their own power.

Character is the highest quest in life. It is the quest for Christ. We will be forever followers of Him. It is a journey that begins without seeing the end from the beginning – but with only the hungry heart to drive us toward "that which is unseen."

*"So we fix our eyes not on what is seen, but on what is unseen. For what is seen is temporary, but what is unseen is eternal."* 2 Cor 4:18

## FAITH, ACKNOWLEDGEMENT AND VISION

Slowly, vision comes. Vision is future potential encountered. When we encounter vision, our perspective shifts from complacence to a holy and spiritual discontent – realizing we are not where God wants us – yielding a new faith for the greater reality.

---

[78] 2 Corinthians 4:17 For our light affliction, which is but for a moment, working for us a far more exceeding and eternal weight of glory

This quest for Christ is based upon the divine call that draws us out of a condition of slavery into a chrysalis of change, which produces what Paul cites as being the New Creation. Proverbs 25:2 says: *"It is the Glory of God to conceal a matter, but it is the honor of kings to search it out."* Royalty is the supernatural by-product of this quest for the character of God and His glory. As we pursue God's glory, we are fulfilling our royal mandate. *"We are a chosen generation, a royal priesthood, a holy nation, God's special possession that you may declare the praises of Him who has called you out of darkness into His marvelous light."* 1 Peter 2:9

Character: born out of the unseen vision that God has placed within each one of us.

Which he calls us to trust

Through covenant and commitment

> To resist unbelief
>
> To occupy

## THE DIVINE PIVOT: FROM TRUST TO ACKNOWLEDGEMENT

To Obey
To Exercise
To Learn
To Give
To Remember (not by might or by power)

## THE MYTH OF THE SELF-MADE MAN

Character is the genius of the divine action and intention carried out in and by the body.

The work by David Brooks, *The Road to Character*, chronicles a number of individuals who, despite their status and position in life, embodied Christ-like character. In one case, Brooks cites NFL Hall of Fame quarterback Johnny Unitas. He allows us "to see" how people of character are often camouflaged by their humility.

"Unitas was not an overnight sensation in the NFL, but he was steadily ripening, honing his skills and making his teammates better... He was loyal to his organization and to his teammates. In the huddle he'd rip into his receivers for screwing up plays and running the wrong routes. 'I'll never throw to you again if you don't learn the plays,' he'd bark. Then, after the game, he'd lie to the reporters: 'My fault, I overthrew him,' was his standard line."[79]

In many ways, those stars of the past lived in a different culture, but they also lived in a different context of character. For me, one of the signatures of character is how they make everyone better. The longer and deeper God goes to develop one's character – the longer and deeper it will last.

*"Then I went down to the potter's house, and there he was, making something on the wheel. But the vessel that he was making of clay was spoiled in the hand of the potter; so he remade it into another vessel, as it pleased the potter to make."* Jeremiah 18:24

"[Humility] if you can't learn it, God will teach it to you..."[80] Frances Perkins Wilson, the first woman appointed to a U.S. Cabinet position.

We have already investigated how Acknowledgement produces heaven's atmosphere within the spheres of our own environment. As we are conformed into His image and character, we are then, through the work of the Holy Spirit, fitly joined together into communities that become the mystical Body of Christ.

## OUR CHARACTERS ARE THE STONES QUARRIED BY GOD

The Acknowledged Life puts together these "building stones of character" from the quarry of sacrifice.

*"The house, while it was being built, was built of stone prepared at the quarry, and there was neither hammer nor axe nor any iron tool heard in the house while it was being built."* 1 Kings 6:7 NASB

---

[79] David Brooks, *The Road to Character*, p. 241
[80] Frances Perkins Wilson was an American sociologist and workers-rights advocate who served as the U.S. Secretary of Labor from 1933 to 1945, the longest serving in that position, and the first woman appointed to the U.S. Cabinet.

It is through our intentional and willful choices that these forces of life produce in us the quarry stones that comprise the temple God is building for Himself.

It is no wonder that our characters become the building blocks, the living stones, containing our values and virtues that are mined through our Acknowledgement of God's purpose.

*"Now if any man build upon this foundation gold, silver, precious stones, wood, hay stubble..."*

1 Corinthians 3:12

The revelation of believers as precious stones is also found in the New Testament in Matthew 16 when Peter Acknowledges Jesus as the Christ:

*"Simon Peter answered and said, 'You are the Christ, the Son of the living God.'*

*Jesus answered and said to him, "Blessed are you, Simon Bar-Jonah, for flesh and blood has not revealed this to you, but My Father who is in heaven.* **And I also say to you that you are Peter, and on this rock** *I will build My church, and the gates of Hades shall not prevail against it. And I will give you the keys of the kingdom of heaven, and whatever you bind on earth will be bound in heaven, and whatever you loose on earth will be loosed in heaven."* Matthew 16:16-9

This is a fantastic example of Jesus finding the rock in Peter. That rock was not only Peter (Petros in the Greek meaning rock or stone), but even more so, Jesus was identifying the rock of revelation as the cornerstone for Peter's new identity.

Acknowledgement begins as we apply the revelation of Jesus to every situation, and in the process God is quarrying the rock of character in our lives.

## THE THEME OF STONES

Stones and rocks are important metaphors in scriptures, especially of Jesus as the corner stone:

*"Therefore thus saith the Lord GOD, Behold, I lay in Zion for a foundation a stone, a tried stone, a precious corner stone, a sure foundation: he that believeth shall not make haste."* Isaiah 28:16

*"And are built upon the foundation of the apostles and prophets, Jesus Christ himself being the chief corner stone;"* Ephesians 2:20

*"Wherefore also it is contained in the scripture, Behold, I lay in Sion a chief corner stone, elect, precious: and he that believeth on him shall not be confounded.:* 1 Peter 2:6

Corner stone: The corner stone (or foundation stone) concept is derived from the first stone set in the construction of a masonry foundation, important since all other stones will be set in reference to this stone, thus determining the position of the entire structure. Today, the corner stone is hollowed out to contain metal receptacles for newspapers, photographs, currency, books, or other documents reflecting current customs, with a view to their historical use.

It was Peter's Acknowledgement of Jesus that set him apart from the other disciples.

This is similar to Mary, when she accepted the charge of the angel, *"And Mary said, Behold the handmaid of the Lord; be it unto me according to thy word. And the angel departed from her."* Luke 1:38 Mary's Acknowledgement of the calling of God in her life, however unlikely it may have seemed, enabled her to become the mother of the Savior.

But perhaps we can look at another believer's case in which there was a bit of a reluctance to Acknowledge what God was about to do.

*"And an angel of the Lord appeared to him, standing to the right of the altar of incense. 12 Zacharias was troubled when he saw the angel, and fear gripped him. 13 But the angel said to him, "Do not be afraid, Zacharias, for your petition has been heard, and your wife Elizabeth will bear you a son, and you will give him the name John. 14 You will have joy and gladness, and many will rejoice at his birth. 15 For he will be great in the sight of the Lord; and he will drink no wine or liquor, and he will be filled with the Holy Spirit while yet in his mother's womb. 16 And he will turn many of the sons of Israel back to the Lord their God. 17 It is he who will go as a forerunner before Him in the spirit and power of Elijah, TO TURN THE HEARTS OF THE FATHERS BACK TO THE CHILDREN, and the disobedient to the attitude of the righteous, so as to make ready a people prepared for the Lord." 18 Zacharias said to the angel,*

*"How will I know this for certain? For I am an old man and my wife is advanced in years."* 19 *The angel answered and said to him, "I am Gabriel, who stands in the presence of God, and I have been sent to speak to you and to bring you this good news.* 20 *And behold, you shall be silent and unable to speak until the day when these things take place, because you did not believe my words, which will be fulfilled in their proper time."*

Luke 1:11

Zacharias was suffering from an Acknowledgement crisis. Not in asking the angel a question. That wasn't the problem, since Mary's response to a fantastic prophetic word was pretty similar. But Mary Acknowledged the word and Zacharias refused to Acknowledge. And this lack of Acknowledgement would have put him in disagreement with God, forcing God to silence him from saying anything about his unborn child.

In looking at this, I point out the importance of Acknowledging what God wants do in our lives. In the case of Zacharias, the angel didn't want Zacharias's words impeding the plan. The point being: **Acknowledgement makes a difference when it comes to your future purposes.** Take a look at Zacharias's response when it came time to name his only son. At this point in the story, Zacharias is still unable to speak. When he is asked about the name for the child, he writes emphatically, *"His name is John!"*

At this point he is able to speak again and is filled with the Holy Spirit and Acknowledges God as such:

*"Blessed be the Lord God of Israel,*
*For He has visited us and accomplished redemption for His people,*
*69 And has raised up a horn of salvation for us*
*In the house of David His servant—*
*70 As He spoke by the mouth of His holy prophets from of old—*
*71 Salvation from our enemies,*
*And from the hand of all who hate us;*
*72 To show mercy toward our fathers,*
*And to remember His holy covenant,*
*73 The oath which He swore to Abraham our father,*
*74 To grant us that we, being rescued from the hand of our enemies,*

*Might serve Him without fear,*
*75 In holiness and righteousness before Him all our days.*
*76 "And you, child, will be called the prophet of the Most High;*
*For you will go on before the Lord to prepare His ways;*
*77 To give to His people the knowledge of salvation*
*By the forgiveness of their sins,*
*78 Because of the tender mercy of our God,*
*With which the Sunrise from on high will visit us,*
*79 To shine upon those who sit in darkness and the shadow of death,*
*To guide our feet into the way of peace." Luke 1: 68*

Not too bad a comeback for a guy who just 9 months earlier was disagreeing with God.

There is an inextricable connection between Acknowledgement and character.

But as difficult as it may appear to be at the time, when we Acknowledge God, it is in anticipation of a manifestation of God.

Just think about it for a second: you don't need to Acknowledge the Verrazano Narrows Bridge before you cross it or even the Brooklyn Bridge for that matter. Why? Because you can see them.

You Acknowledge God because you CAN'T SEE HIM OR THE BRIDGE OR THE CHILD OR THE RESOURCES that appear to be missing.

Acknowledgement is like saying, "I've got an appointment to keep. God is going to show up and I need to be there when He arrives."

As the revelation of Jesus as the corner stone of the church takes shape, there are other stones that go into building the temple of God. There is this significant and meaningful connection between Rocks, Revelation and Manifestation.

## OTHER INSTANCES OF A STONE AND REVELATION

Jacob slept on a rock before he realized that where he slept was a ladder that reached heaven:

*"…and he took of the stones of that place, and put them for his pillows, and lay down in that place to sleep. And he dreamed, and behold a ladder set up on the earth, and the top of it reached to heaven: and behold the angels of God ascending and descending on it."* Gen 28:11-12

The Hebrews were in a desert where there was no water, and Moses produced water from a rock: *"Behold, I will stand before thee there upon the rock in Horeb; and thou shalt smite the rock, and there shall come water out of it that the people may drink. And Moses did so in the sight of the elders of Israel."*
Exodus 17:6

## DAVID CONQUERS GOLIATH

*"And he took his staff in his hand, and chose him **five smooth stones** out of the brook, and put them in a shepherd's bag which he had, even in a scrip; and his sling was in his hand: and he drew near to the Philistine."* 1 Sam 17:40

Paul reveals the Rock that followed the Israelites: *"And did all drink the same spiritual drink: for they drank of that spiritual Rock that followed them: and that Rock was Christ."* 1 Corinthians 10:4

The rocks of revelation, the rocks of testimony are following us in the same way that they followed them. The difference between those wayfarers and us lies in the area of realization. We must embrace, make way and Acknowledge the Rocks of Revelation that Abraham, David, Jacob and Peter lived by.

God has even hidden our kingdom name on a rock:

*"He that hath an ear, let him hear what the Spirit saith unto the churches; To him that overcometh will I give to eat of the hidden manna, and will give him a white stone, and in the stone a new name written, which no man knoweth saving he that receiveth it."* Rev 2:17

But in order to see the rocks of heaven, God requires that we live The Acknowledged Life.

"*Therefore thus says the Lord God, 'Behold I am laying in Zion a stone, a tested stone, a costly stone, for the foundation, firmly placed. He who believes in it will not be disturbed.'*" Isaiah 28:16 NASB

## PRAYER
Build us up, Lord, into Your likeness, with Your character for Your purposes. Let nothing interfere with this holy work.

## Chapter 15

# ACKNOWLEDGEMENT, OUR SLINGSHOT OF INFLUENCE

## ACKNOWLEDGEMENT

My Acknowledgement makes my ordinary obedience and excellence extraordinary in the hands of God. And because I live an Acknowledged Life, He can trust me in the big battles that will liberate people to enter into their promises.

## KEY POINTS

* I only surrender to Christ, the Cross and the Kingdom. Everything else I overcome by the Blood of the Lamb, and the Acknowledgement of my Testimony, and I don't give up
* Because I am not in control, it allows God to be in control
* The circumstances may be new to me, but they are not new to God
* Today, as I Acknowledge Him, I get to walk in His Victory again

*Influence is acquired in the valley of adversity.*

By the title of this chapter, we could be tempted to believe the 'slingshot of Influence' is a fast-track or shortcut to success. Not so – there is no shortcut. The slingshot is not so much a surefire way to accelerate one's promotion; rather it represents a primitive and less-than-agile means to accomplish a supernatural outcome.

From the Bible's perspective, adversity should be viewed as a crucible of transformation. It is the proverbial telephone booth we enter as a mild-mannered reporter for a great metropolitan newspaper, and then emerge, through the power of God, as superman (see chapter 3), accomplished through the work of the Holy Spirit.

Our culture extols control as the prerequisite of success, but biblically, we are taught to learn to be content and to trust the Lord with all of our hearts.

We face thousands of decisions every day; some are automatic, like breathing, blinking, or what shoes to wear, and then there are those decisions that are based upon our character and values.

There is a right way and a cheater's way of navigating adversity. The cheater's way is to avoid by any means the decisions that cost us, delay us or deprive us of the things we are striving for. The right way or the winner's way is to address the 'threats' through instruction, application, and diligence.

There are typically 3 means by which adversity arrives at our doorstep:

Hereditary or pre-existing
Predatory or combative
Developmental or instructional

Adversity may also come through a combination of all 3.

Our first instinct when encountering a form of adversity is most often to see it as a foe. It is our natural tendency to interpret any difficult or uncomfortable condition as adversarial and poised to oppose our progression. I would suggest our own subjective cognitive process is the primary impediment to overcoming an adversarial condition.

## ADVERSITY THROUGH HEREDITY OR A PRE-EXISTING SOURCE

My grandmother, Tate, as we referred to her, encountered a number of pre-existing conditions. She was born in Homs, Syria. She immigrated to America in 1917 and found work in a factory as a seamstress, ultimately marrying the boss. Unfortunately, the Great Depression came, and her husband lost everything. Tate went back out to work in a factory, doing what she had to do to survive.

When she arrived here in America, she couldn't speak English, but over time, becoming widowed by the death of my grandfather, Tate learned to save her nickels and pennies and some dollars. She eventually bought a building on Third Avenue in Brooklyn. Then she bought a second building on Narrows Avenue. In a few more years, she bought two more buildings. Tate didn't interpret her story as being a victim, but rather, she used adversity to bring out the real estate mogul hiding inside of her.

## PREDATORY OR COMBATIVE ADVERSITY

God permits adversity. If God allows anything, God has a reason. Sometimes what we think is an advantage becomes a disadvantage – and vice versa. What happens when you do the right thing and the wrong thing happens?

A biblical example of spiritual combat occurred when David heads out to deliver some food for his brothers fighting the Philistines, only to discover they are cowering under the threats of this gargantuan giant called Goliath. David ends up defeating the giant using a sling and a single rock. Yet, instead of garnering the love of the king who sent him to fight the foe he was unwilling to confront, he ends up a fugitive from his king himself. The king actually commands a proactive campaign to kill David.

David needed to learn a spiritual lesson: You rarely win against the giants by playing small ball. When it comes to spiritual warfare, it is never a fair fight. That is because God has a higher purpose in mind; spiritual victories have spillover effects. David defeats Goliath, the Philistines are defeated. A young boy with 5 loaves and 2 fish gives what he has to Jesus, and everyone gets fed.

If adversity is predatory or combative, the source is spiritual, and you cannot engage it at the level it comes to you. David chose not to fight Goliath using Saul's armor; he went out in the power of God to defeat God's foe. *"For the weapons of our warfare are not carnal, but mighty through God to the pulling down of strongholds."* 2 Corinthians 10:4

## DEVELOPMENTAL OR INSTRUCTIONAL ADVERSITY

When I first started working on the floor of the New York Stock Exchange in 1981, few people I met down there had graduated college, and if they had, it was a mere formality, as they were given positions in their family's brokerage firms. I had no idea how the market worked and what the sequence of terms meant. It was as hard as learning a new language: it was English but not English that I ever heard spoken.

The culture clash was very intense. There I was, a college grad, yet I was ignorant, and everyone made me feel ignorant. What I then determined to do was listen to what was said, and repeat it to myself, like I was practicing scales on the piano. He said, "A half, three-quarters, 5,000 by 2,000, ten grand ahead, and Morgan Stanley has a working order for 25 not-held."

It took a while, but I learned it. Finally, one day, it clicked and I understood what they were saying and even more, what it meant to the orders that we were handling. It didn't come at once, or twice or even the third week, but in about 3 months, I was understanding what was being said.

The adversity of my own ignorance introduced me to a new language I would use for the rest of my life. I learned more than the language on the floor of the New York Stock Exchange; I learned that if you want to take a territory, you have to learn to speak the language.

## THE CHEATER'S WAY AND THE RIGHT WAY

The cheater's way is to sidestep or even ignore problems: health conditions, financial, relational, occupational and other difficulties. Initially, we interpret the arrival of adversity as something to be circumvented.

However, the right way to get through your adversity is not to ignore the lessons embedded within them. Rather we should look to understand them as a laboratory of transformation, beginning with changing your perspective to uncover the opportunities, causes, effects and answers you have overlooked.

How do you see adversity? As an obstacle or as an opportunity?

What something produces in our lives depends on perspective. In other words, if you are looking at adversity as an opportunity for things to go wrong, they probably will. If you are looking for problems, they will appear. On the other hand, if you are looking at adversity as an opportunity to learn or grow, you may find not problems but possibilities for promotion.

## MASTERS OF ADVERSITY

One of the greatest students of adversity was Thomas Edison. He had trained his mind never to interpret 'failure' or defeat as conclusive. For Edison, failure was simply a course in the educational university of life.

Edison's success in management of crisis produced an indefatigable character that would never relent until he accomplished what he set out to do.

Thomas Edison's teachers said he was "too stupid to learn anything." He was fired from his first two jobs for being "non-productive." As an inventor, Edison made 1,000 unsuccessful attempts at inventing the lightbulb. When a reporter asked, "How did it feel to fail 1,000 times?" Edison famously replied, "I didn't fail 1,000 times. We now know 1,000 ways not to invent the light bulb."

## CITY ON A HILL

Acknowledgement injects God into circumstances. When Thomas told Jesus, "Lord, we know not where you are going; how can we know the way?" Jesus told him, *"I am the Way and the Truth and the Life."* John 14:5-6 Acknowledgement is God's pathway through adversity to influence. We were all created to release the influence of hope, life and power.

Earlier in the book, we discussed the revelation that the Lord is about 'mining' in us the rocks of revelation as He did in Peter. These rocks are the words the Lord has excavated out of us to be revealed for His purposes. **When we operate in purpose, we exercise influence.**

The Puritan John Winthrop is the one who helped to frame the phrase 'City on a Hill' referring to America. He understood this aspect of Acknowledgement; the purpose of the Puritans within the purpose of God. Often, God allows adversity to force a movement or a change we interpret as inconvenient or an impediment to transformation.

In the case of John Winthrop and the Puritans, their persecution in England and the physical challenges of establishing a community in the New World produced a clarity of vision that would define this unborn nation as a bedrock for the dissemination of the Gospel.

The colony struggled with disease in its early months, losing as many as 200 people to a variety of causes in 1630, including Winthrop's son Henry, and about 80 others who returned to England in the spring due to these conditions.

They were to be an example for the rest of the world in rightful living. Future governor John Winthrop stated their purpose quite clearly: "We shall be as a city upon a hill; the eyes of all people are upon us." The *Arbella* was one of 11 ships carrying over a thousand Puritans to Massachusetts that year.[81]

Winthrop could not have imagined the impact this country would have upon the world and the Gospel. Who knows what would have happened if England's religious climate were not as hostile to the Puritans as it was, forcing the Pilgrims to venture to the New World.

**Convenience, comfort and complacency ultimately become the opponents of the purposes of God.**

---

[81] https://en.wikipedia.org/wiki/John_Winthrop

Until this day, America is not only that city; it has continued to reflect the light, the reality and the hope of the Gospel to generations, despite its imperfections. The way that you interpret adversity will either contribute to your influence or detract from it. As in life, you are either growing in influence or losing it.

## THE RELATIONSHIP BETWEEN ADVERSITY AND INFLUENCE

Inventors appear to be a unique breed of people because of their ability to withstand setback. Among the many innovations that Thomas Edison was involved with over the course of his life was the battery.

During the first decade of the twentieth century, Edison spent much of his time developing a storage battery that he intended for use in electric automobiles. Edison had a long-standing interest in battery design dating back to his time as a telegraph inventor. But that pursuit encountered an adversity anyone else would have deemed to be insurmountable.

One of the landmarks of his efforts is the building in West Orange, New Jersey known as the Battery Factory [which today some developers are flipping into residences]. In 1914, the Battery Factory survived the massive fire that destroyed Edison's laboratory complex. The Battery Factory survived due to one reason: it was constructed with Edison Cement, a building material Edison invented for its resilience.

Edison's response to the massive fire was, "I'll start all over again tomorrow." The interesting thing about this was Edison was 67 at the time. Considering the average life expectancy was 52 back then, it is a pretty bold statement to make. He not only came back but he 'saw' the firefighters' efforts were hampered by the lack of visibility (there were no street lights) and the preponderance of thick, dark smoke. So within 48 hours of the fire, Edison invented a powerful battery-powered searchlight.

Edison did not let the clouds of adversity hamper his creative ability and consequently, he was able to apply his knowledge of batteries for automobiles to the invention of the battery flashlight.

## THE PRINCIPLE OF INFLUENCE

The principle of influence is found in its power to illustrate, demonstrate and communicate a preferred action to solve an issue or problem.

As we learned, we are tempted to believe we can achieve what we want through a shortcut called knowledge or information. As was proven to be the case in the Garden of Eden, knowledge is one of our erroneous zones.

The second erroneous zone is related to influence. As Jesus taught, we are to be salt and light: AKA influential.

The problem is two-fold: First, we were born with a condition known as sin, which affects our cognitive capacity,[82] and second, as Paul explains to us, *"For now we see through a glass, darkly."* 1 Co 13:12 This relates to our perceptive or sensory capacity. The old expression holds very true here, "We don't see what we don't see."

So why would God choose to make us both in His image and likeness and with a mandate to rule? Our spiritual continuity requires not only an alignment with God's plans and purpose, but depends on our reliance upon Him, "For without me you can do nothing."[83]

## GOD WANTS TO GIVE US MORE

Even Moses, who was living in the house of Pharaoh, was not released into his call and influence until he had submitted to the process and crucible of the wilderness and caring for his father-in-law's sheep.

But ultimately, Acknowledging God is intended to enlarge our field of vision, or to produce authority and influence in order to accomplish the purposes of God.

---

[82] "For my thoughts are not your thoughts, neither are your ways my ways, saith the LORD." Isa 55:8
[83] John 15:5

## THE ACKNOWLEDGED LIFE

## UNLIKELY WEAPONS OF MASS DELIVERANCE
In order to underscore His signature and involvement, God uses simple, often primitive devices to unleash the grandiose glory of heaven. Slingshots, rods, packed lunches and cords are truly unlikely weapons of mass deliverance, except in the Bible.

## MY STORY ON THE NYSE
Back in '81, when I started working at the NYSE as a clerk, I thought I was 'good to go' as far as my career was concerned. Well, not only did I learn the business; I also learned something about myself: I had a small case of dyslexia, which is not always a fatal condition – except when you are dealing with millions of dollars and a small slip can cost hundreds of thousands of dollars.

Well, this led to a conversation between me and God, where I did most of the talking. I told Him, "If You were going to send me into the belly of the financial beast, at least give me the gift for numbers! But NO! How do You expect me to function? Is this any way to run a Kingdom?"

What this condition did was force me to work extra hard, get there on time, and stay late. It also gave me the chance to help with some operational systems that were adopted throughout the NYSE Floor. But operational excellence was not going to be my slingshot. No, all that time it was a character-producing process that God was interested in.

It taught me God is laser-focused on character before achievement. What I did as a clerk was "my slingshot." What I did as a clerk was to create a coded system for orders that nearly eliminated the incidence of confusing institutional buy and sell orders. The system was adopted across the entire exchange, saving probably millions of dollars in errors.

*"Reputation is what you send ahead of anywhere before you arrive."*

As we Acknowledge God in our lives, He begins His work of sanctification and consecration, which results in our personal spiritual authority.

Paul writes in Ephesians 1:7, *"God did all this, so that in the coming ages he might show the immeasurable riches of his grace in kindness toward us in Christ*

*Jesus."* God saved you in order that He might demonstrate something. He wanted to demonstrate the immeasurable riches of His grace and kindness.

It is not YOUR grace, riches and kindness; it is His!!! Our part is to accept God's No's for our lives so that we are prepared for His Yes's.

Someone who conquers the impossible will always leverage greater influence than those who simply do the possible.

When David slew Goliath, he slew a perception that stood taller than the six-foot, six-inch stance of Goliath. Goliath overshadowed the destiny of a nation.

Perhaps the greatest and most formidable foe we will ever defeat is that of a perception: the perception that cancer is final, that race is a liability, that intelligence accounts for the final grade or that our age or origin will determine just how far we can go.

As we begin to understand when we Acknowledge God in any of our 5 fields, we are placing God over our conditions and environments, our wildernesses, our identities and now over our characters. Then we will and should expect to see God move in totally dramatic ways.

"Today average is officially over. Being average just won't earn you what it used to."[84]

The New Testament states, *"But you are A CHOSEN RACE, A royal PRIESTHOOD, A HOLY NATION, A PEOPLE FOR God's OWN POSSESSION, so that you may proclaim the excellencies of Him who has called you out of darkness into His marvelous light."* 1 Peter 2:9

These days, I believe the Lord will not be slinging stones, building arks or bringing wise men from the east to get His point across. He will be redefining what it means to be 'an average Christian.'

I look upon the spiritual discipline of Acknowledgement as David slinging stones while shepherding his father's flock. Acknowledgement is done in private every day. No one really sees you doing it every day.

---

[84] Thomas Friedman, "Average is Over" Part 2, *NY Times*, August 7, 2012

So answer this question: What do David of the Bible and you have in common? What are the stones God has given to you to sling? David changed his nation with a slingshot.

Acknowledgement is a biblical skill that once understood, applied and maintained can change a course, a condition, or a calamity into conquest.

*Chapter 16*

## INVITATIONS

I like to think of life as a party. Great parties are few and far between; they get remembered and talked about for years and generations to come. As with any party, preparation is important, but the secret to any successful party comes down to your guest list.

Acknowledgement is how we put God on the top of all of our parties: our marriages, businesses, families, and communities. The ministry of Jesus began with a party: a marriage. Having Jesus at that marriage reception made all the difference in the world, especially when they ran out of wine.

I remember this wedding Carol and I went to; they barely had enough food. It was winter, the hall was cold. Everyone was just sitting at their tables; no one getting up, no one moving, even though the disc jockey was playing music. No one was dancing.

The Lord told me to get up and dance. I didn't want to but heck, I was so bored that I dragged Carol onto the dance floor and we started dancing. Now I am not really much of a dancer, I'm more of a mover. And the only dances I could remember were from my youth: The Twist, The Jerk, and The Monkey. I started dancing, and all of a sudden people started getting up to dance, until the floor was filled with people. That is when the Lord said to me, "Do you know what they are thinking?" and of course I didn't. "They are thinking, I can dance better than he."

The next day, after Sunday service, I was walking down the stairs with Jusup, an Indonesian worship leader at our church. We said hello to each other. He was at the wedding the prior night. Then he said to me, "You know, last night I danced with my wife for the very first time. Men and women don't dance in Indonesia. But last night that all changed. Do you know why?" I said, "No?"

"I saw you dancing and I said to myself, 'I can dance better than he can,' and so I got up with my wife and we danced."

The wedding turned out great, but it came down to the guest list, starting with Acknowledging Jesus – on the dance floor in this case.

Just remember, whenever you Acknowledge Jesus, you DANCE.

"I hope you never lose your sense of wonder
You get your fill to eat but always keep that hunger
May you never take one single breath for granted
God forbid love ever leave you empty-handed
I hope you still feel small when you stand beside the ocean
Whenever one door closes I hope one more opens
Promise me that you'll give faith a fighting chance
And when you get the choice to sit it out or dance
I hope you dance
I hope you dance"

"I Hope You Dance" Lee Ann Womack

If you are breathing, it is because you are still **at the dance called life…and no one knows how to dance better than God!** We are here because our lives are worth it. Your journey and value begin with Acknowledgement and learning to understand the road signs God has given each one of us.

God loves comeback stories. We are all in one phase or another of a comeback; but it all starts with Acknowledgement:

## PRAYER

I Acknowledge You, God, in this day; that without You I can do nothing, but with You and through You I can do anything. Thank You for today, it's Your gift to me that I give to You. I pray for Your favor to be on me, this day and the works of my hands. Let today be a parable, a proverb and a miracle for me and all those around me.

So you don't have to wait for an invitation: God's put an invitation into your hand through this book; and I hope you will dance!

## ABOUT THE AUTHORS

Anthony DiMaio is a business blogger and brand specialist who married his Brooklyn Tabernacle sweetheart, Carol. For many years they lived in Manhattan, but now call the Jersey Shore home. He has facilitated thousands of meetings throughout the city and for years has threatened to write a book. He is the coordinator for the NYC marketplace ministry, BOLD Ministry, which was founded by Tim Keller and Gordon MacDonald. He has worked with and mentored many individuals across all industries to help them recognize their true potential and apprehend vision for their lives, families and businesses. *The Acknowledged Life* is his first book of many, which will not take as long to write as *The Acknowledged Life*.

Vaughn Weimer, CFP™ has spent 40 years as a financial adviser, volunteer for not-for-profit organizations working on Wall Street, and serving since 1998 on the board of directors for the Bowery Mission. Vaughn and his wife, Joann, live in Long Island and have 3 grown sons. He is also on the pastoral team at his home church, Mosaic Vineyard. He and his wife are passionate to see lives transformed by the power of God's kingdom. Vaughn and Anthony have collaborated on several projects over the last 40 years.

Made in the USA
Lexington, KY
06 March 2018